**She Is Well**
Stories of Power |Strength |W
Volume 1

Copyright @ 2021Women Wellness Lounge
Published by TLC Publishing Company
Brandywine MD 20613
www.tlc-publishing.com

Book Layout & Formatting by TLC Publishing Company
Library of Congress Cataloging-in-Publication Data is available upon request.
ISBN: 978-1-64999-098-3
E-Book ISBN: 978-1-64999-099-0

Printed in the United States of America

## Disclaimer

Although you may find the stories and advice to be useful, the book is sold with the understanding that neither the authors nor TLC Publishing Company, are engaged in presenting any legal, relationship, financial, emotional, or health advice. The purpose of this book is to educate and entertain. The authors and publishers shall neither assume liability nor responsibility for anyone with respect to any loss or damage caused directly or indirectly by the information in the book.

Any person who is experiencing financial, anxiety, depression, health, mental health, or relationship issues should consult with a licensed therapist, advisor, licensed psychologist, or other qualified professional before commencing into anything described in this book.

# She Is Well

### Stories of Power | Strength | Wellness

### Volume 1

*www.sheiswellbooks.com*

### Presented by Delayna Watkins

**TLC**
PUBLISHING COMPANY

www.tlc-publishing.com

# Table of Contents

# Introduction

**W**elcome to the She Is Well Tribe! This book project is for every woman on the journey to becoming "She" from everything that has come before "Her". The initial idea and concept for this book project was supposed to be birthed as a solo collection of my nuggets to becoming well in every area of life. But through my conversations in the Women's Wellness Lounge, I realized that other women needed to share their voice and tell their story. I feel blessed to extend this contributing author opportunity to include other women because it will have a greater impact. Being obedient and listening to God has taken this project deeper and wider than I could imagine.

I dedicate this book in honor and memory of my beautiful mother, Sandra Marlowe Queen. A Queen that spread love with her very presence!

Thank you to every woman that believed in my vision and said "yes"! We are now the She Is Well Tribe!

She Is Power. She Is Strength. She Is Wellness.

Special love and gratitude to my husband Tommy Watkins and our beautiful children, Tenae, Breona, Thomas, Reggie and Brice.

# Foreword

## PRESENTED BY DR. RICA WILSON

Collective stories are the salve of our community. We are either birthing our own stories or marinating in midwifery while our sisters are pushing through the pain to breathe new life onto their dry bones. Have you ever had a valley experience? Where did you turn during your lowest moment? Reading has a way of taking folks on an unforgettable journey. Sit-down. Relax a moment.

We are sisters- words that have refused to drown in the midst of the valley. Our words have emerged out of the deep and dark corners of our broken hearts. We are multicolored shiplap-unshackled ancestral chains seeking freedom. We are freedom-words unbound by invisible heavy chains. This midnight sun rocks our hearts to sleep like a newborn baby waiting for daylight to appear behind the shy mountains. Indigo blue and purple emotional rocking chairs only stop singing slave riverbank songs when we lift our heads and open our eyes.

When winning is losing, you think differently. You realize that it's not about what you've lost, but what you've found. Can you imagine finding gold-real gold at the bottom of a pile of trash. No, really think about digging into a pile of smelly trash infested with flies and maggots only to find real treasure at the bottom of the pile. Regardless if you selected your pile of trash or not, life happens. No one is exempt from experiences that shake us to the core and rock our foundation. Resilience is what you practice when you are standing in the middle of your pile of trash. When you realize that you are greater than the trash-like experiences that you encounter, you win. The lessons that you learn while in the bottom of the pile will propel you into the next level.

Sure, experiencing heartache and heartbreak is not fun. The good news is embedded in what happens after your storm. Yeah, pressing play after the storms of life is not easy. However, the storm strengthens your spiritual muscles and improves your core. Do you really think God would set you up for failure? God loves you. Some women may have tears still falling while reading the stories of the women in this book. It's okay. It's okay to cry. It's okay to laugh. It's okay to heal. Lift your head. Stand tall, and dust yourself off. You made it, and this book may be the puzzle piece that you need to heal.

Do not worry if you are struggling with mental illness, depression, rejection, abandonment, or anything else that makes you feel less that than the masterpiece God created. You are loved. You are a treasure, baby-girl, and if someone missed the opportunity to love you right, it's their loss. Stop crying. Stop worrying about the future. Stand still in your blessing of now. Now you are here. Now you have the opportunity to heal. Now your pain has positioned you for your purpose. What are you going to do with your now?

Yeah, what happened hurt. Yes, what is happening is hurting you, but there is hope. You are still beautiful. You are still strong. You are enough. Get your mind back. I know the pain can be overwhelming, but you still have the chance to make another choice-a positive choice. When you get your mind back, you make a conscience decision to delete every message from your mind that is out of God's will for your life. You can choose to play another recording in your head. You can begin to speak kindly to yourself. You can rest when you are tired. You can say no without apology. You are obligated to take care of yourself because you recognize your value. Getting your mind back requires commitment and consistency. It may not happen overnight, and that's okay. The joy comes with the journey. Imagine if you gave yourself the love, care, time, and commitment that you have given to people who hurt you-those who may never appreciate or celebrate you. Can you make a choice to choose you? Choosing you requires you to get up from your dark place, look yourself in your pretty bold eyes, and proclaim: I choose you, beautiful because you are worth it.

I need you to vomit your truth. No, don't swallow the deafening silence and choke on lies meant to crush your soul. Yes, vomit. Allow the chunks of negatively, hurt, and years of abuse to propel from the little girl deep inside who was wounded long before a man had the opportunity to break her heart. You know her. Tell her it's okay. Let her know that she did not do anything wrong. Hold her hand. Let her know that you are letting go of secret's that adults and other folks forced you to tuck into the pit of your little girl stomach and heart. It's over. The moment you selected

{5}

this book and opened the first page, the shift began to happen. Keep going. Allow yourself to remember, to feel, to heal.

When you vomit your truth, you realize, feel and know there is nothing pretty about your pain. However, there is something pretty about a woman who can walk out of a fire without her head lowered in shame. There is something beautiful about a sister who refuses to concede to defeat regardless to her hardships. Beauty is getting up after getting knocked down over and over again and making the choice to trust God and be still until the promise manifests and moves you into your destiny. It's not over. Your story is just beginning. God loves you so much until he revised your life. Now you are in a position to bless other women with your story. Open your mouth. Feel the words dancing on the city pavement or country roads.

Watch them jump double-dutch on clay dirt in rural communities. Watch your words swim across the Atlantic to get the freedom your ancestors only imagined. Do that. Open your mouth, swallow your pride, open your heart and read. Connect with the women on the banks of this reading river. This healing tribe is standing in the warm blue-black water with you. We refuse to turn our backs on you-especially not now. Turn the pages. Let's walk together, heal, and get our woman freedom. It's the kind of freedom not written in historical documents or captured on wooden coins. Your future is bright!

You are stronger than you know. Your strength comes from knowing- knowing you are special and you are enough. Sure, you will have moments when you want to look back, but don't. Keep going. Your freedom is forward. Love is not about winning with others. Love is about knowing and loosing, so you can find your true treasure-yourself.

Trust God. Get your joy. Demand your peace. Turn the page, sis! Welcome to your next chapter!

Delayna Watkins is a true Wellness Mayven with a real passion for women's wellness. As a board-certified registered nurse with extensive clinical and leadership experience, Watkins is recognized in the industry of health and wellness. Receiving the Governor's Citation award for her work in the healthcare field, being a best-selling author, and nursing leader all represent her dedication to women's wellness.

Delayna, most notably is the CEO and founder of the Women's Wellness Lounge™, an intimate space where she provides health advocacy and lifestyle change services to thousands of women locally and nationwide. She recently expanded this concept and launched a national TV Show and Podcast the

*Women's Wellness Lounge Show* which provides education and entertaining content for women.

Delayna has also created the **Sugarless Living Program™** which is a result driven program responsible for helping women and their families decrease their consumption of refined sugar and processed food, leading to weight loss and diabetes prevention. As a speaker, Delayna is authentic, electrifying and energetic. Her delivery shifts the audience into action and provides support for immediate lifestyle change.

Since pursuing her passion Delayna has been recognized and featured on various national platforms and media including the Dr. Oz Show, Fox 45, The Steve Harvey Morning Show, Wealthy Sistas Radio, Diva Zone Magazine and other professional networks. She has provided services for University of Maryland, National Black Nurses Association (NBNA), Coppin State University, National Association of Professional Women (NAPW), Internal Revenue Service (IRS), and many other professional organizations.

Delayna remains in hot pursuit of her dreams and goals with the unwavering support of her family and she is honored to be a voice for women to experience total wellness at any age!

# Being Well
## in the Midst of Grief and Loss

On a beautiful and unusually warm November morning while driving to meet with a client, I made a phone call that changed my destination and life forever. I was simply calling to get an update on my mother's condition. Sounds of praise and worship were playing in the car while I patiently waited for the nurse to come on the line and give me a report about how Mommy was doing. Instead, I hear the voice of a male who identified himself as her doctor and immediately my heart sank because I knew something was terribly wrong. The praise and worship music became faint, the beautiful sun faded behind clouds, and my voice began to tremble as I asked what was going on with my mother. The doctor explained that my mother had just went into cardiac arrest and they were actively performing CPR! My heart began racing and my breathing became intense as I yelled at least three times "keep going, I'm on my way"! Although he couldn't explain how my mother's condition became so critical, he agreed to continue his life-saving efforts until I arrived. I called my sister and as my voice was cracking, she knew right away that something was wrong with Mommy. She was closer to the hospital so I yelled for her to get there NOW to be with Mommy because I didn't want her to be alone during what would become her last moments alive!

The sudden and unexpected passing of my beloved Mother, Sandra Marlowe Queen thrust me into a world of functional grief. She was just one day shy of celebrating her birthday when she suddenly transitioned without warning. I needed and wanted more time but, in my heart, I knew that my last visit with her the evening before would become part of many cherished memories and moments spent with her. After hours of reasoning, bargaining, disbelief, and shock, I mustered up some strength to wipe away tears while simultaneously entering a dark place where I would meet grief head on!

Right away I knew that I wasn't going to get along with grief. The way we met was not on my terms and we weren't properly introduced. Yet suddenly grief was a part of my life and would be there for quite some time. I remember thinking, I didn't have time for grief because my family, friends, co-workers and supporters wanted to know what happened to Mommy and I had to share the details of what happened. I explained the scenario so many times it began to actually feel real with each narration. I don't remember falling asleep the first night, so I think mental exhaustion must've kicked in and took me out of my misery. I heard my Mother's sweet, angelic voice telling me that everything would be fine as long as I didn't give in to the strength and power of sudden loss and grief. I woke up and started bawling my eyes out yet again but those tears were cut short since my phone wouldn't stop ringing. Grief had to wait a little longer.

While grief was waiting to hang out with me, I started planning Mommy's homegoing celebration. Thank God for the many friends that I needed and wanted to stay by my side throughout the overwhelming planning process. There was so much to do through the unbearable pain and sometimes uncontrollable tears. As the eldest child I knew that I was responsible, I just wasn't prepared and expressed on several occasions that I wanted this to all be a bad dream. I was mentally exhausted and physically weak as I mustered up the strength to push through the details necessary for a memorable celebration to honor my mother's life and legacy.

## The Hidden Crisis

My heart briefly filled with joy after my mother's homegoing service because I knew with 100% certainty that she was remembered and honored like the true loving, kind and caring Queen she was here on earth. Then suddenly, I was thrust back into "grief mode" again as soon as the noise of people filling my home, calling my phone, giving me hugs and sending me love began to fade away. My mind began to hang onto the sudden loss and absence of my mother which caused me to fluctuate between confusion, anger and sadness. I didn't realize that this was the beginning of a hidden crisis. I said "hidden" because it wasn't something that could be seen with the naked eye but it was brewing inside. I was putting on a façade with my family and friends that I was coping with my mother's death. I appeared strong and was seemingly "handling it well" or "the best that could be expected" was how it was described. Little did anyone (myself included) know that I was a ticking time bomb, and the worst was yet to come.

When we think about grief we often think of the tears, the anger, and the guilt. We talk about the strain it puts on our relationship with friends and family. We consider the existential crisis it can induce. But one thing that often doesn't get discussed is that grief can bring on physical changes created by our relationship with food. For most people this means struggling to eat anything, with a stomach in knots from pain and anxiety. For others, grief and comfort eating become a constant reality. My grief had suddenly introduced food as another new best friend. The scenario happens suddenly but feels gradual and goes a little something like this: you are feeling sad, depressed and alone, your favorite pizza from the neighborhood carry-out sounds good and you begin licking your lips and thinking about the soft crust and all of those cheesy toppings. Oh, and don't forget that you can't have just one slice. Not to mention how you'll wash it down with a cup of cold, sugary, delicious iced tea or a glass of red wine… it all depends on just how sad or depressed you're feeling. Well, this was my reality for roughly six months following my mother's death. My eating habits became so unhealthy I somehow convinced myself that it wasn't so bad and I deserved to eat what I want because of what I was going through… you know, my mother just died and my heart still hurts. At some point, I realized that I was eating my grief and not dealing with my emotions at all! I had gained well over 18 pounds during the time that I was hanging out with and getting to know grief. Once again, my family and friends didn't notice a thing because I was "doing fine" and still worked out almost every day. So yes, it is absolutely true that you can't out exercise a poor unhealthy diet!

Now, those of you who have spent any time following a healthy trend or a weight loss regimen have likely experienced some food-and-beverage-splurges now and again. Sometimes that bag of salty, crunchy potato chips or soft and creamy ice cream is crucial for a proper day of sulking. However, those splurges can turn into daily events when you're grieving. Before you know it, your pants become too tight, you're eating a pint of ice cream a day, you feel like crap, and you see that it's a vicious cycle, but you still can't seem to get it under control.

## Crisis Management

Why do we change our eating habits when we're grieving? Good question! It's called comfort eating. There are actually a number of reasons grief and comfort eating go hand-in-hand, which is probably why it is so common. We all want to be happy and feel a sense of bliss in our lives. Positive things and creative magic happen for us and those connected to us when we're feeling good and not consumed with sad thoughts brought on by grief. Comfort eating makes us feel good and keeps us coming back for more so we can stay in this happy place. What is going on in our brains with food is pretty similar. Food, especially fatty or sugary foods, triggers the reward system in our brains. We start firing all those feel-good neurotransmitters, like dopamine, and our brain is telling us to just keep eating all that delicious, fattening, sugary food. You're probably thinking, "I shouldn't be eating this" as you grab another handful or swallow the last spoonful of deliciousness. You are not going crazy and there is a clinical explanation for what you're experiencing. It's referred to as the 'stages of grief' and I first learned about it in nursing school. We had to memorize the acronym D-A-B-D-A (denial, anger, bargaining, depression, and acceptance. But what I've learned since my mother passed away suddenly is that the stages of grief can actually be defined by how and what you eat. And guess what, there are 5 stages of 'grief eating' that you experience through the process.

## Stage 1: Eating nothing

There's a funny irony in the immediate post-death phase: During the time when your grieving is at an all-time high, you don't feel like eating anything, yet your fridge is overflowing with food. Heaven forbid you go to a mourner's house without a dish of food! I remember we had more grilled chicken, turkey, biscuits, cakes and pies than any one household could handle. Most of our family and friends brought some of my mother's favorite dishes as if she were there to enjoy them. I didn't really eat any of it although every dish looked and smelled delicious. My nearly month-long grief diet consisted of a few bananas with an occasional avocado and egg toast sandwich. Months later I was still finding food that had been lovingly wrapped up in my freezer. Who knew chicken and biscuits would freeze so well?

## Stage 2: Eating anything

This is the stage when you realize that you are left alone more often, which means no one is watching. Cookies at 8 a.m.? Why not! Eating a whole pint of ice cream in one sitting? Oh yeah, I did that a few times. It's like my stomach was happy to be receiving regular nourishment even if it wasn't healthy. It was all working perfectly until I started feeling sluggish and it became harder to resist the sugar cravings or the urge to splurge. Most often more than half of grieving individuals stay in this stage until they realize what appears as sudden weight gain. Followed by a phase of vigorous exercise to boost their mood and help lost the weight. So, this stage is where I spent most of my time grief eating and rationalizing.

## Stage 3: Eating just one

One piece of fish. One slice of pizza or one whole pizza. One carrot, or sweet potato, or taco. It was during this time that I began to compromise with food. I knew I had to eat, but not too much. So, I consumed enough to keep me going without gaining more weight. I think the quote that less is more would really describe how I was feeling about food around this time.

## Stage 4: Eating out

I remember the first time I went out with friends after my mother's death. We were a group of five, and as I walked in and saw everyone sitting at the table I almost ran out of the restaurant. Knowing that social isolation is the alternative to going out, I forced myself to enjoy the company but truly thought about just asking for my meal to-go. Someone must've known I would run for the door, so my seat was in the middle of the table which had me surrounded by some of my best girlfriends. The grilled salmon, veggies and cheesecake for dessert was absolutely delicious. Something was beginning to happen, and I felt proud at this point because it was my first healthy meal eaten outside the home with someone other than my husband.

### Stage 5: Eating with no regrets

Finally, there's a point at which food becomes re-normalized. Sure, I have my days when that almond butter jar gets a workout, but mostly the crazy ups and downs of my food journey have stabilized, about as much as my grief has. There has been one major change, though. In all parts of my life now, I try to be open to new things—in this case, to break out of the routine of the same foods, restaurants, and experiences that defined my life.

I've always been a very healthy and routine eater. The joke in my family is that I'm just waiting to become a mermaid in my next life because I eat so much seafood. Certainly, I had very black and white views on food. I like this. I loathe that. But like with everything in my life now, I'm trying to look at things from a different perspective, and in this process, I've learned that apparently, I do actually like brussel sprouts, red wine and gouda cheese—all foods that for years I avoided like the plague!

After a short time on this food/grief journey, it became clear to me that the way forward is to understand the emotional relationship with food throughout the grief process.

**What to do if you are comfort eating your way through grief:**

☀ **Pay attention to your triggers.** Paying attention can help you find patterns in your over or undereating. The easiest way to do this is to keep a detailed food journal to include when you eat (time and date), what you eat, how hungry you were when you started eating (on a scale of 1-10), and how you were feeling when you started eating and when you finished. This can help you identify times, places, and emotions that may be triggering comfort eating.

☀ **Consciously consider whether you are actually hungry.** So much of our eating is from habit, comfort, and simply wanting to eat. More than likely there are emotions driving you to seek food. This is where I use the HALT method to determine true hunger because you may be Hungry, Angry, Lonely or Tired. Consider before eating anything how hungry you are. If you are scoring yourself low on the hunger scale, find an alternative to eating.

☀ **Know your alternatives to eating.** I know, trying to think of an eating alternative when all you really want is a slice of pizza or cheeseburger with fries seems impossible. But having a plan for when you want to eat but aren't really hungry can help. Some options are:

☀ Make a cup of tea, then reassess if you really need to eat something.

☀ Do some deep breathing. If food is a reaction to a spike in stress or anxiety for you, sitting down and doing deep breathing for a minute is proven to lower cortisol levels and can help put a break between you and that food you might not really need.

☀ **Learn to tolerate tough emotions**. If you realize that emotions are triggering, you're eating, this is often a sign you are avoiding the emotion and trying to sooth with food. Rather than avoiding these emotions when they come up, take the time to experience them. Find ways to express the emotion through writing, reading, or another outlet that works for you. Learning to tolerate these feelings reduces the tendency to avoid emotions with food and helps us find alternate ways to cope. At this stage in my grief process, I created a rule about avoiding emotions. I gave myself permission to feel EVERY EMOTION at ANYTIME! Even it meant crying in the middle of the grocery store (which I've done several times) or pulling into a parking lot to cry and scream, or randomly laughing aloud as I remembered something about my mother.

☀ **Practice mindful eating**. For me this is one of the best habits you can adopt. This is the simple practice of making sure you focus on, notice, and savor every bite of your food. Take the time to look at your food and smell it before you take a bite. When you put your food in your mouth, notice the flavors and textures. Chew each bite thoroughly and notice it as you swallow. Thoughtfully take your next bite, repeating this as you eat. Practicing this can help you assess whether you truly want to eat something, whether you are truly enjoying it, and to stop when you are satisfied. Many people realize they are satisfied with much less food than they would normally eat, and that some foods are not appealing when more attention is paid to the experience of eating them.

☀ **Find other pleasures.** The sad reality is that when we are grieving, much of the joy is sucked from our lives. It is not uncommon for people grieving, or people suffering from depression, to identify food as one of the few pleasures they currently have. If this is the case, it is crucial to seek other pleasures and rewards that work for you to replace food.

☀ **Get help.** Sometimes these tips just aren't going to be enough. If you are still struggling with grief related emotional eating, consider a counselor or group therapy to further explore your grief and relationship with food.

It is possible to grieve in a healthy manner. You must identify healthier ways to grieve after a loss and give yourself permission to heal. My mother loved to cook, and her delicious food always brought me comfort. Now I've learned to allow the beautiful memories of my dear mother to comfort me.

Mom, your legacy of love carries me through every day, and I miss you dearly!

Dr. D. Rica Wilson has been an advocate for human rights and education for most of her career. Wilson graduated from St. Augustine's University in Raleigh, North Carolina with a Bachelor's degree in English. She has a Master's Degree in English, with an emphasis in teaching English as a Second Language, from Indiana University of Pennsylvania. She holds a doctorate in Pastoral Counseling and a certificate in Complementary and Alternative Medicine. As a licensed minister and law student, she blends compassion and cultural competence to seek justice for voiceless and vulnerable individuals. Dr. Wilson is the founder/executive director of Brown Girl Wellness Incorporated, a non-profit organization that strives to empower marginalized women and children.

She enjoys cooking, traveling and spending time with family and friends. Wilson is a member of Alpha Kappa Alpha Sorority, Incorporated.

# August

*Blessed is she who has believed that the Lord would fulfill his promises to her! (Lu. 1:45)*

People don't really tell you what happens when the smoke clears. The pain doesn't just disappear into thin air like a puffy rain cloud. The hurt lingers like an open wound with white puss and redness all mixed up in emotions. The dust settled, but the hurt would not move for years. Seemingly, each time that I saw him or heard his voice, I remembered.

I was transported back to moments of momentary happiness and sadness. I saw my little green car parked in the first vacant spot at the police academy. I saw him running laps in his grey academy jogging pants and racing for the finish line. I recalled the days that I drove miles just to give him a hug in the small college town. My mind took a trip down memory lane to movies and basketball, but my heart wouldn't stop aching. Where was the man who unlocked my heart? With each memory, my heart cried a little as she remembered the broken promises and harsh words that ripped polished hardwood floors and granite countertops in our first house. Well, I thought it was my house. While living in apartments, I spent years paying the bulk of the bills, so he could save his paychecks to purchase us a home. He told me that he had a plan, and I believed every word. Why would he lie? He loved me-right? He wouldn't allow me to pay the bulk of the bills and take the money that he saved for the house. We were building together, right? I moved into the house bit by bit. The day that I turned in my apartment keys was bitter-sweet. I could not shake the feeling in the pit of my stomach. Finally, I moved into the house, but my stay was brief and chaotic. His words became shorter and cut deeper each time he gazed at me with a cold and distant look. Slowly days and nights blended because his late arrivals from work turned into not coming home at all. Despite the frost of the ice palace, I was certain that it was my home until I found out that my name was not on the deed. After I spent years supporting us, he took his paychecks and invested in himself; I did not own anything. He did not include my name on one document; I didn't have a house after-all. It all began to make sense, but not make sense. I recalled text messages, lonely nights, hot tempers, and awkward silence. The day that I began to face the slow truth, I was devastated. Unable to stop the tears, I just let the tears flow onto the steering wheel as my heart tried to reject the betrayal. He had another life. How did I miss the signs? Some folks think the love just goes-fades away like fog or morning mist, and maybe so for some, but not for me. The love lingered, and soon enough I gave myself permission to feel-really feel because they were my feelings, and I did not owe anyone an apology for loving another human even if they didn't love me right. Most importantly, the moment that I acknowledged my love for him instead of trying to hide it underneath the brown fall leaves, I could love myself better. I loved. I really loved him, so everything that I gave him in love was not a loss. The tears watered the seeds that I planted in love. It was a gain, and God would honor my truth.

After the smoke cleared, I only had one penny left in my bag. I can't quite remember the color of the bag, but I knew what I could do with the penny. I looked into the room and saw my boys sleeping in the only bedroom in the warm apartment. The high ceilings and windows gave me hope. I could see the moon peeking into the dimly lit space, and it created a bright space inside of the loft apartment. Whatever would become of the penny needed to happen quickly. My boys needed food, school clothes, pencils, and lots of love. Of course, they had love, but after all of the difficult days, they needed a little extra. I searched for hugs and kisses to soothe their pain and mend our hearts. Their walk-in closet was the perfect space to create a wonderland. I used the teddy bears and toys to create the ultimate escape for them. I started having family fun night each Friday to help them smile. Despite the toy wonderland in the closet, my heart broke a little more while standing in the doorway. The big soft brown teddy bear and Talking Elmo could not erase the events that lead us to this moment. Deep inside I knew that what they saw and heard would impact them, but I prayed that they would not remember. It seemed like I stood in their doorway forever that night, and I could not catch the tears fast enough. What happened? Why was this happening? This was not the picture that I painted as a little girl. Where was the neatly painted family picture-the one with the smiles? This was not what I expected. I loved him. Maybe I loved him more than I loved myself during those difficult moments. Somehow, I would always remember the way that he walked into a room with his Timberland's hiding beneath the denim. I held onto the times when he kissed me every morning before his shift. Each happy thought was clouded by memories of unkind words and actions that tried to rip my self-worth from my soul. He loved me-right? He didn't mean it. He had a bad day. So, I tried to love him more, but nothing changed. Why wasn't my love enough? I continued to watch my boys as they slept, and I hoped their minds would erase every bad memory as they slept peacefully-innocence untouched.

I walked over to the stairs of my loft apartment, placed the penny in the corner near the wide landing, prayed and wrote a long letter to God detailing our needs. This step was my new praying place. This was it. I could pour my heart out to God here, and it was my safe place. I just tucked my head into my brown tired arms and cried. I cried because he didn't love me, and I cried because I didn't love myself the way that I deserved to be loved. Did I miss something? Did I not love him enough? Why was this happening? It wasn't that bad-right? Were the years of supporting his every desire in vain? I folded his clothes, made sure his meals were hot and awoke long before daylight to iron his uniform. Maybe that's where I went wrong. Why was I folding his boxer's anyway? He wasn't treating me like he loved me, but I just kept giving and giving while ignoring who I should've been loving-me. I searched for answers. Were the silent stares and harsh words really all that remained after I gave my all? For the next few days, I walked by the penny and the letter while telling God thanks for answering my letter.

I continued to move about my day in faith. Finally, I drove to the local social services office. My boys were in the car, and I wanted everything to seem normal. I sat there for several minutes before actually walking inside. The walk from the car to the front door of the building seemed like a million rotating winters. The heavy electric door didn't seem to work. Maybe that was my sign to leave. I continued to think about returning to the car. I began to think about the summer that I met him again. I was sitting on a wooden bench like the one across from the parking lot. The paint was peeling, but no one noticed. The only difference was the bench adjacent from this building was a make-shift bus-stop bench. Spray paint covered the kinda round shelter just above the bus-stop bench. I don't know if people really cared about the bus-stop, the shelter, or the tattered bench. The bold words written in red paint showed disrespect and abandonment of appreciation. After-all, where would people sit if there was no bench? Where would they go if the devalued curbside bus shelter didn't cover them from the rain? At this point my life resembled the makeshift bench more than ever. The torn boards were my twin somehow. All of a sudden, the black electric door with the cloudy glass opened. I walked inside, signed in at the table with the security woman and strolled over to the cold pale seats. The security woman never looked up. Was this normal? Her uniform said it was just a job. The crossword puzzle under her pen agreed. Her off brown hat was covering her brown eyes as she held her head low while waiting for folks to enter and exit the building. Were people invisible here? The corner to my immediate left had a few disheveled coloring books and broken crayons. I directed my boys to the corner with some familiar items. As they colored with the crayons, I returned to the pale seat and began to cry. I thought of my multiple college degrees, the way that I had always worked at least two jobs, and how much I fought to escape poverty. Despite my best efforts and having a top HBCU on my cv as a former place of employment, Professor Wilson, me-was sitting one the social services office waiting to apply for food stamps. There was no hilltop, no greeks were gathered on the yard, there were no buildings named after playwrights and literary craftsman and writer women-word carpenters who made words tap dance and roll their hips at the same time. Food stamps-really, I asked myself. How did I get here? Seemingly, just yesterday day I was an aspiring future law school student waiting to change the world. Did love really do this to me, or did lack of love for myself do this to me? The embarrassment engulfed my pride, I watched my boys color with the broken crayons, sat in the pale cream chair, and continued to cry silently. I began to feel more and more overwhelmed. How did I get to this point? How did I fail myself? I looked at my naked ring finger and wondered what really happened. The questions bombarded my mind, and just before they called my name to walk behind the light brown wooden door to see a case worker to apply for food stamps, God whispered, "broken crayons, still work". I tried to compose myself while gathering my sons, but the tears would not stop. God was right. I thought I was humble before, but my heart was not. Something inside of me broke that day, and my not-so humble heart has never been the same.

I was approved for food stamps, and the $125 helped me budget like never before. Between my makeshift job, and the food stamps, we had what we needed. I didn't eat out, cooked cabbage and rice at least three times a week, and saved a few dollars to make my boys sweet potato pie on Friday's.

Every Friday, they took their little red chairs, sat in front of the stainless-steel oven in our one-bedroom loft apartment and smiled at the stove while watching the sweet potato pie bake. Their smiles while looking at the oven with such sweet anticipation blessed my soul. I knew then like I know now that things would get better.

Sure enough, God answered my letter. One single letter changed our lives. The college that I applied to several months earlier made me an offer, actually I received offers from one local college and a major university within the same week. I took the job closer to our one-bedroom apartment. Afterall, it exceeded the salary that I asked God for in my letter. I had all the benefits that I could imagine and more. This was our fresh start. The sting of being told to leave our 4-bedroom house with the cute porch and cherry blossom tree didn't feel so bad since I had an offer to re-build our lives. Sometimes the tide changes in August.

For I know the plans I have for you," declares the LORD, "plans to prosper you and not to harm you, plans to give you hope and a future.

Are you experiencing an August shift in your life? Are you feeling broken? Is your heart aching from betrayal or abandonment? Have you allowed someone's negative words to stick to your soul like glue? If so, I am excited about your future.

What if the experience was your ultimate set-up by God for you to step-up your game and become refined for your purpose? What if the thing that did not break you was really your work-out to make you stronger? What if your valley is the step before your victory? Can I challenge you for a minute? Girl, I dare you-I double-dog dare you to get low in your valley. Lean over the dry bones in your life, and speak over yourself. Speak to every dry place in your life; tell it to live. Command every dry bone to get up. It's not over. Yes, you heard me right. It's not over! You are still here. You are still purposed for greatness. You did not begin reading this book by chance. Every page that you have turned thus far is not a mistake. You are here because this book is your healing place. As you are turning the pages, pages are turning in your life from sadness to joy, from lack to overflow, from why me to why not me. Right now, this book is your prayer line. At the moment, this book is your little wooden prayer bench that sits in the front of Baptist churches in the deep country-benches waiting for broken hearts to kneel-this book. I'm believing God for your breakthrough. I'm standing on the sidelines cheering for you as you walk towards your freedom. It's not over!

I dare you to tap into your So What! So, what things have not worked out like you expected. So, what folks have shattered your dreams and expectations! So, what they have walked out! So, what! Find your Now What! Now what are you gonna do to love yourself? No what are you going to do to heal? Now what are you going to do when you find yourself in the middle of your August with just one shiny brown penny? Believe. Pretty woman created by God, believe. Watch your prayer work and the sun peek from behind the clouds in the middle of your midnight hour.

You are loved. You are enough!

So, if the Son sets you free, you will be free indeed.

John 8:36

Single Mom of 4, LaTalya Palmer is here to serve! She has gone from generational welfare to 6 figures; from incest survivor who hated herself to an empowerment specialist helping Women Build their Confidence, IGNITE their Magic and Manifest their Dreams!

LaTalya is an International Bestselling Author, Speaker, Founder of Phoenix Rising Success Coaching and Training, Certified Peak Performance and Law of Attraction Coach.

She was a teen mom that stopped attending college to raise her family; a generational welfare recipient that abruptly walked away from welfare at a young age vowing to find a better way; participated in a Welfare to Work program and learned how to break into and thrive in the workforce. She used her gifts and resources to become a Welfare to Work Trainer and Case Manager then a Family Development Trainer, training Front Line Human Service Workers, Directors, and Supervisors.

LaTalya lives with her children in Maryland and is committed to helping women IGNITE their passion and manifest their goals-NO MATTER WHAT!

# You Have the Power to IGNITE Your Dreams—Despite the Adversity

## Storms will come...

For the first time in years, I felt optimistic again. It was January 2017 and despite my divorce 5 years prior and the loss of my mother 2 years earlier, I was determined to come out on top. I declared that 2017 was going to be my year! There were goals and dreams lying dormant in me and I was ready to bring them forth. I committed to finishing the book that I started writing 3 years prior; I started going to psycho-therapy; began eating healthier as I gained a great deal of weight, had high blood pressure and high cholesterol; I began dating again; I was finally taking care of my needs and it felt great! I had my share of despair and adversity, but I held the faith that I would heal. I had hope that even after all the pain and detours, my dreams still had a chance to come to life.

But that momentum was short lived and came to a halt in July of that year. I felt a lump. I tried not to scare myself and be a downer, but it grew, and I grew more fearful. I also developed an aggravating pain under my left arm. And by August both became unbearable and I drove myself to the emergency room. I tried to stay calm in the waiting area but couldn't help but to worry over what could possibly be growing inside of me, causing me so much pain. The sonogram they administered that night didn't provide any answers, the imaging was too dark. The experts didn't know what they were looking at. Thus, the doctor referred me to a breast surgeon for further testing. And, so began the grueling road to diagnosis.

Over a two-month period, I endured multiple biopsies, lump drains (the doctors thought the lump was a cyst) and sonograms. Each time they drained the lump, it would grow back larger. It took intense advocacy to get the necessary tests administered. Sometimes bringing friends and family members to my appointments with me for help. I had a difficult time trying to talk to the doctors while simultaneously process what was happening to me. I kept pushing for them to give me the appropriate tests to see if I had cancer. The health insurance company needed more justification to determine whether they would pay. My sister provided me her research of our extensive paternal family's history with breast cancer. I passed it along to my doctors. Eventually in October, they gave me an MRI and PET Scan.

On October 13, 2017, I was diagnosed with advanced Stage 3, Inflammatory, triple negative, breast cancer. It was highly aggressive and inflammatory breast cancer is rare. By this time, the lump grew from 2 cm to 12 cm, the cancer invaded the skin on my breast-turning it red/orange with enlarged pores, it invaded my lymph nodes and was eating through my pectoral muscle. If they didn't act quickly, it threatened to make its way past my chest muscle and spread into the rest of my body. The weight of the lump on my breast kept me in constant pain. It became unbearable, and it looked as if I had a third breast. I just never thought I would hear the words, "You have cancer". It was a grim diagnosis and I felt lost and confused. There was no way that my life could end just like that! There was still so much life to live. I was only 43. My children still needed me. I had dreams in me that were not realized. I finally finished writing my book and was ready to hit the 'publish' button. This could not be the end. Not this way. Not now.

People close to me did their very best to keep my uplifted, but the truth was, it was devastating for me and extremely hard to wrap my mind around. I didn't know what was ahead of me, but I knew I had to quickly gather myself and prepare to fight. I remember telling a close sister-friend that if I die, it won't be because I didn't fight. I was very much aware that God gave me life. I was resentful at the thought of something taking what's mine and was adamant that cancer could not take my life. I was sure that this was not the way He wanted my life to end.

## Claim what's yours...

The fight began with reclaiming my mind. I had to get clear, refocus and make healthy decisions. Although I gave myself permission to cry, it was imperative the I did not lose myself in the tears and grief. The first decision I made was to live. I was clear that there were too many things undone and too many experiences unfulfilled. The second decision was to change my diet-my cousin told me to change my diet immediately. The weight gain, high blood pressure, high cholesterol and cancer were evidence of weakened immune system. It had to be strong enough to fight the cancer and withstand the chemotherapy and radiation. The third was to publish my book. In 2014, my mother asked me when I was going to write my own book. I promised that it would by March 2015. She died March 2015 and I hadn't kept my promise.

## This time, I was determined to keep my promise

The diagnosis came on a Friday and by Sunday-in the midst of the tears and panic- I had a rough draft of a vegetarian meal plan, started to search for alternative doctors, gained additional information about inflammatory breast cancer, and hit the publish button on my first book. I built up enough fortitude to see the dream through. I looked cancer in the face and said you will not take this from me and self-published the book 2 days after my diagnosis. And to sweeten the victory, my tribe rallied around me to ensure I had an official book launch one week before starting chemo.

No matter what you are facing, no matter how out of control your circumstances seem, there is always an opportunity to claim what God gave you. You are not lost, and you are not alone. You can claim the very breath you breathe, and the very thoughts you are thinking. Your breath is life and your thoughts are creative in nature. Both are extremely powerful, and they are your own to gain control of.

I learned how to take what's called 'full conscious breaths' from a great teacher. She taught us to breathe in for 4, hold for 7 and breathe out through pursed lips for the count of 8. Four rounds of full conscious breaths will relax your mind and open it to think more clearly. Once in a clearer state of mind, ask God what to think and set your intention. A panicked mind can't help you make the right decisions. A limited and fear-based perspective can't help you see your way through. Ask for guidance and the steps to move you forward. Listen to and trust your intuition. From that space, stake claim in the promises that God has for you and the dreams you have for your life. Then, no matter how small or big, take the steps to bring them into fruition.

## Staying the course...

To stay the course and ignite your dreams despite of the adversity, you must determine for yourself- why it's worth the fight. Through the experiences of my hair falling out, losing my breast, weakened body, multiple surgeries, scars on my psyche and body; caring for and healing myself while supporting my children emotionally; grieving; learning that my sister was diagnosed with breast cancer and the BRCA 1 gene one month after I was diagnosed and not being there with her; learning that my daughter has the BRCA 1 gene and so much more- I was still determined to stay the course. I asked myself, was I going to give in or was I going to fight and thrive? I looked in my children's eyes and made the decision to fight and thrive.

Staying the course, requires that you get still, listen, learn, and implement. I recognized early in life that illness showing up in the physical is a sign of what was going on internally. For me, cancer was no different. I knew that I had healing on all levels to do. In addition to my prayer, meditation, and guidance from loved ones, I sought out information on emotional healing. I researched and learned that issues with the left breast were an indication of the need to heal maternal issues. The tumor represented hardness, lack of forgiveness, resentment, and the need to love and embrace myself. There was a great work to do, it was challenging but I was ready.

Igniting your dreams during or after times of adversity require a vision and mental toughness. Even if you don't feel that you don't have anything to look forward to, trust that you can shift your mindset one thought at a time. Your will-to-win will develop as you walk your journey. Encourage yourself and understand that your dreams may be on pause momentarily but the obstacle is not an order to cease and desist. While it may seem impossible to focus on your goals while enduring a painful experience, know that as your drive and determination grows, so will your mental muscle.

Have a vision and something to look forward to. During my treatment and surgery phase, I also completed a Law of Attraction Coaching Certification Program. I needed to refresh my coaching certification and needed the mastery skills to help me build strength and create a new vision of myself. The certification and mastery of coaching was a compelling enough vision to help me see beyond the diagnosis.

You may not have a life-threatening diagnosis but whatever you are enduring has a toxic element that, like the cancer, is eating through your dreams. Know that you have a power within and around you that is greater than any obstacle you encounter.

Tawawn is the CEO/Founder of TL Consultancy, LLC, an author, certified life coach, change agent and speaker. TL Consultancy, LLC is a woman- and minority-owned multifaceted company based in Maryland which is the umbrella for the Women Walking in their Own Shoes™ Movement and Foundation.

Tawawn has blended her Bachelor of Science – Behavioral Studies degree, change management and Myers-Briggs practitioner certifications, and over 25+ years of professional experience to deliver a little TLC to her clients. She empowers **individuals and organization with driving change to achieve transformation and success.** Through transformational lifestyle coaching, consulting and content (TLC), Tawawn inspires and equip individuals to make significant shifts that lead to life-changing transformation, maximized potential, translate visions into goals, and goals into successful outcomes. She provides services to organizations leadership to bringing forth sustainable change, empowering people, leveraging talent, and achieve results.

**Tawawn's Why**... For more than half her life, Tawawn believed her life had no real purpose. See she turned somebody else's limited belief about her potential into a self-fulfilling prophecy, making it true. She secretly lived an unhappy and unfilled because she believed success could not be a part of her story.

Her goal is simple, to give everybody she encounters a little transformational lifestyle content (TLC). The TLC needed to help bridge the gap for where you are, and want to be.

# Empty Cradle, Shattered Heart

## YES, YES, YES!!!!!

That was my answer. How could it have been anything other than yes. I had always dreamed of this day. It was one of my biggest dreams coming true. My yes would be one of the most important decision I made for my life. Saying "YES" was getting me one step closer to my heart desire. I felt the favor of God in my life. He had heard my cries. His word says, He will give you the desires of your heart. I had been dreaming of this moment for a very long time. While it didn't happen the way I envisioned it, it was happening.

It all started with a phone call. It is amazing how one phone call can change your life. I often wondered how different my life may have been, had I not taken the call. Or if I had just said no. While this was something I dreamed of and desired. I knew this decision would require a lifetime commitment and responsibility. I was hopeful that all my soul searching, open mind and heart would be enough. August 10, 1998, about 2:00ish, I remember it like it was yesterday. When I heard his voice, I could feel the butterflies in my stomach. The husky deep voice I heard so many times sounded so serious. When he said "hello Ms. Harrison, this is Mr. Brown from the Department of Health and Social Services". I knew then, this was the moment I had been waiting for. Because I was so deep in my head, I didn't respond immediately. When he said hello again, he had my full attention. What came out his mouth next was my miracle. I had to ask him to repeat himself again. He proceeded to say, "we have a 1-day old baby girl abandoned by her mother in the hospital 1-hour after giving birth. We are terminating the parent's rights, and we need an adopted home for her, would you be interested?" I could not believe my ears, and without hesitation, or thought, I said yes. How could I not. A newborn, girl, again my prayers was being answered. While I was excited. I had one hundred and one questions for Mr. Brown. Mr. Brown answered all my questions, and everything was favorable. His very last question, "would you like to come up to the hospital today and meet your daughter?

I was so excited that I couldn't contain myself. This one phone call, and my yes had instantly changed my life. I was going to be a mother. I called my mom screaming with delight letting her know she was going to be a grandma, told my supervisor, put in my leave slip, and made my way to the hospital. As I held my 6lbs 10oz bundle of joy, I counted all her fingers and toes, and immediately fell in love. I wondered how could someone abandoned someone so precious. My heart was full of gratitude. Everybody said adopting an infant through social services would be impossible – but when you serve a God who operate in the impossible. I was 31-years old, and my desire to become a parent had yet to happen. So, this opportunity to be an adoptive parent was a dream come true. I was given a girl child – Woo-hoo; and my goal to adopt was being achieved. Becoming an adoptive parent had been a goal since I was 16-years old. Yes, at 16-years old I had decided that I want to be a foster or adopt a child. It was at that age that I learned that two of my girlfriend's mother wasn't their biological mom. She was their foster mom. I really didn't understand what that meant then, but I knew because of Ms. Barbara Jean, my girlfriend's lives was no different than mines. She had changed the trajectory of their lives. So, I made up my mind, that I would be a foster or adoptive parent when I grew up.

After meeting my daughter and talking to the doctors, I spent the night on my face thanking God for His favor, and this blessing. The two days following I spent meeting with doctors, social workers, visiting and holding my daughter. My family and friends were awesome. They jumped in and helped me prepare the nursery and get my home ready. Over those two days I learned there were no family members on either side willing to take the baby. The birth mother had named her before leaving the hospital, but I would be able to re-name her (immediately), the court date to terminate the parents right was in place (within 2-weeks), and that my baby girl was healthy. By the way, I named her Taylor Alexandria Harrison. Taylor's life was already blessed prior to me bringing her home. A good girlfriend blessed me with a beautiful crib and changing table; and a friend of my hairdresser gave me two large green trash bags full of new cloths with tags on them.

On day four of Taylor's life, all the preliminary paperwork to make her temporarily mine was complete. We were headed home to become a family. Taylor's presence brought immediate joy to my family. My mom and grandmother were just as enthusiastic to have her apart of our family. Like any other new mom, I took maternity leave, my job and family gave me a baby shower, and I had a new normal. A week after I brought Taylor home the craziness started with the biological parents stating that the hospital stole their baby. The thought of losing Taylor was heartbreaking, but that drama was very short lived. The process for terminating the parent rights went off without a problem. Things was progressing well, and I was happy. I was no longer holding my breath waiting for the worse to happen.

Well, the worse happened. This would be another phone call to changed my life. An aunt from Taylor's father side had learned about her and decided she wanted custody. When the social worker first told me of the aunt I just prayed, and continued to trust God. Day, weeks and months went by, and we heard nothing more about the aunt. Then that dreaded day came that instantly broke my heart. After six months of caring, loving, sleep deprivation (Taylor crying every night from 8:00pm-9:00pm) and watching her grow was coming to an end. I was given a date and time. Just like that, I was no longer a parent. My child was being taken away from me. As my family and I prepared for the day, I could feel my heart breaking in pieces day-by-day. On Taylor's last day with me, that morning I packed her baby bag, and prayed over her. I asked the God who brought this gift to me to keep and watch over her, and I ended my prayer with why? On one of the worst days of my life, I handed my child over to the social worker. As I watched the government car pull off, it was like watching a scene from a movie. That evening I had a physical therapy appointment. When I walked into the appointment the physical therapist asked, "where's my little pumpkin?". I didn't know how to respond. I had only told a few people about what was going on. I don't think

I ever responded to her question. As she massaged my back and neck, the tears flowed like a river. My heart was shattered, and I didn't know how I was going to make it through.

It is a very odd place to be in grieving a child that was yours, and very much never yours all at the same time. My heart ached and I missed her. I had no grave site to visit like parents who lost their child through death. All I was left with was pictures and memories. The depth of my pain was debilitating, and grew worse each day. I couldn't eat, sleep, focus, or find any peace. I blamed myself for putting my family through such an awful loss. I questioned whether I should even call Taylor my daughter. I didn't know how to tell people what happened. Or how to respond when asked how is your baby? I wondered if people would dismiss my 6-months of parenting Taylor. I wasn't even sure if people really recognized my loss. Did my situation fit with the type of experiences and grief of those parents who lost their child through death? I didn't know how to tell people what I was feeling about this entire experience. There were no words for this level of heartbreak.

The first three months after Taylor left was fuzzy. My new normal was work and back home, when I could get out the bed. I spent every night in her nursery crying myself to sleep. I would sit in the rocker, and just look at her picture or hold her favorite teddy bear crying wondering why. The day Taylor left, I stopped praying and speaking to God. I could not understand how he could bless me, and then take the blessing away. My mom would always say, God don't put more on you then you can bare. To this day I can't stand that phrase. While I knew it to be true, I didn't want to hear that shit, at the time.

Losing the opportunity to be Taylor's mother was a significant loss for me. I was an adoptive parent forced into grief and despair because of a disrupted and failed adoption, who didn't know how to grieve a child who had not died but was no longer with me. Our relationship was obliterated by a system who thought it was better to put Taylor with a family member, instead of the person who brought her home from the hospital and cared for her the first 6-months of her life. I hated the Department of Health and Social Services (DHS) system, they had taken away my ability to be Taylor's mom. The world had accepted her as my child, but the reality was no legal system had given me the term "parent". I was merely Taylor's temporary legal guardian. For a very long time I questioned, what was I to Taylor. I felt used by a broken system who didn't care about the people's lives they were destroying. Needless to say, my desire to adopt again was no longer a goal. Losing Taylor made me realize that people didn't see my pain.

One thing that I recognized was people didn't understand the depth of my pain. Unlike death, people didn't come around and check on me, bring food to the house, send cards or flowers, or call. My grief was only acknowledged by immediate family, and just a few close friends. First, I thought they didn't know how my family was suffering from this loss. I realize that people were sad for me, and that they just saw it as bad luck. My family was hurting, and my heart was aching for so many reasons. I don't know when the pain started to get better, but for the first 5-years afterwards, I cried during Taylor's birthday week. When I drove passed the babysitter house. When I saw a pregnant person, or walked down the baby aisle in a store. I cried because I would not see her graduate kindergarten, high school, go to prom, fall in love, graduate college, or any other significant life moments. I cried because I knew she was out there, and I couldn't hold her, nor see her. My godmother stayed in touch for a couple of years with Taylor's aunt, but I could never bring myself to reach out. Every time I thought I was ready I talk myself out of it. How would I explain giving her back? Who would they tell her I was? How would I handle seeing my baby thriving without me?

Needless to say, I was depressed. So, the first step to my healing started with counseling. I was fortunate to find a very good Christian grief therapist who didn't compare or categorize my unique situation. The first question she asked, "what are you feeling?" I told her my heart was heavy. The heaviness from all of the broken pieces that I didn't know how to put the pieces back together. My sessions were always good, but I always left more emotionally drained. I appreciated having a safe place to vent, cry, and just talk about the loss. It didn't take long for me to realize I was grieving more than the loss of Taylor. Losing Taylor brought me face-to-face with my infertility. Adopting Taylor took the focus off that BIG problem. God had given me the opportunity to become a parent, so not being able to biologically give birth no longer mattered. Counseling also help me realize that I still had unresolved abandonment issues. Why did everybody I love leave me?

Counseling lasts a little over 3-months. That when I accepted this was a pain I would need to learn to live with. You never get over losing a child, you just learn to deal with it. I still woke up every day angry and mad at the world. I questioned God and wondered why He gave me the desire of my heart, if He was going to let it shatter my heart. I blamed myself because I should have known it was too good to be true. All along I knew this possibility existed. It has been almost 20+-years and I still grieve the loss of Taylor. Over the years I have navigated every stage of grief. The stages have been fluid and didn't come in any particular order. Sometimes I experienced multiple stages at once, and I learned just because I went through one, didn't mean I wouldn't go through it again. I remember thinking I had finally reached the acceptance stage, then one of my girlfriends announced she was pregnant. I immediately found myself smack dab in the middle of the anger stage.

I finally accepted the fact that Taylor belonged with her biological family, and it was selfish of me to want to keep her from her family. I forgave myself because in my bargaining, I blamed myself for taking the risk. I knew adoption was risky, but I was so focus on becoming a parent. Forgiving myself was a big part of my healing. I was holding myself hostage for bringing that type of pain into my life. Forgiving myself allowed me to release the guilt. Life is about risk, the only one who knew how this would turn out was God.

Grieving a failed adoption is real. The reality is that you will grieve forever. You will never get over it, but you can learn to live with it. Eventually if you give yourself permission, you will heal, and you can move forth from the loss. This chapter of my life started with a yes and ended with a yes. In giving myself permission to heal, I was saying yes!!! Yes, to a mended heart, yes to forgiveness, yes to let go of guilt, yes to not being stuck, yes to being a vessel God could use, and yes to being free from the emotional and spiritual warfare/pain. I had made another life changing decision. I loved Taylor, and she will forever be in my heart, but I also love me, and in loving me, I had to give myself permission to be happy. Happiness did not mean I didn't miss, nor love my baby.

Grieving is a process, and the only way to navigate the process is to go through it. There are no five or ten steps of going through grief. Everybody's process is unique, and personally designed just for their situation. The best thing you can ever do is allow yourself to feel the pain, acknowledge your hurt, and give your pain to God. Trust me I know there will be times when you don't think God is in the midst of your grief, but only He can help you come through.

When I finally started talking back to God, I asked Him why again. As usual, His response was perfect. "He said, Taylor's mother abandoned her 1-hour after giving birth. She didn't get that instant love, snuggles, hugs and warmth that mothers give their newborn. I wanted her to experience the normalcy of a home and family, and I knew you would love her unconditionally". God helped me understand my purpose in Taylor's life. He reminded me why I wanted to be an adoptive parent. He used me to give her normalcy in the first 6-months of her life; and that I did.

Grief after a failed adoption is just as hard as the loss of a child through death. We all love, and we all hurt when that love is lost.

*Tawawn Lowe*

Kimberly Cleveland is The Good Thing Guru, speaker, blogger, event producer and mother to a handsome teenage son. I am the Ladies Ministry Leader and a platform speaker for ladies' programs for over 15 years. As a marriage and wife coach, I have counseled and helped prepare women to become amazing wives with successful marriages. Marriage, being a wife and a mother are my passions! Not so long ago I took a leap of faith and found purpose through my passion and started Wife University! As your coach I can support and help prepare you achieve your dream of becoming an amazing wife and help you create a successful marriage.

Like so many women I asked myself: Why was my dream of being a wife and mother so hard to attain and sustain? I had a career but it wasn't fulfilling. So, I sought the answer from someone wiser than myself .... I got on my knees and prayed.

What I received was more than I asked for. I received clarity for myself and a charge to equip others like myself. God revealed I had spent most of my life educating myself and preparing for a career but had not done nearly as much work preparing to be a wife. For the next seven years, God revealed His divine plan for marriage and gave to me a systematic educational process that transforms a woman into a wife! This gift from God has become The Wife University and I have pledge to God to honor His gift by helping prepare women to become amazing wives!

# The Power to
# Be Resilient in A Season of Chaos

Have you ever had a season in your life when you knew you were being tested? When you are in the boxing ring of life and it has you in that corner. You are stuck with nowhere to run. Life is now going for the knockout. A left punch, no problem. You can take it. Then a right punch. You stumble from the sting of the pain in your jaw. The pain is unbearable. But if life had thrown you two punches at different times or even one after the other and stopped, you might have been ok. But there is something about the one, two, three punch combination that just takes you down. Have you ever been there?

My one, two, three punch was dealing with divorce and depression while struggling as a single mother to raise a son with ADHD. I was overwhelmed. Overwhelmed with trying to pick up the pieces and move forward after divorce. Consumed by the pain, the shame and the guilt which lead to depression. As if dealing with all of that wasn't enough, I was 7 months pregnant and I had to begin my motherhood journey alone, depressed and trying not to be consumed by the devastation of it all.

# THE GOOD NEWS

Divorce, depression and being a single mom raising a child with ADHD almost took me out. BUT GOD. In the midst of the chaos, I found the power to be resilient. Resilience is defined as a person who is able to withstand, recover, bounce back, or adapt quickly from difficult conditions. I want to share my resilience journey with you, with the hope that my story and the steps I took, will motivate, and equip you in your season of trials. Prayerfully, it will provide you the inspiration to push through and know that your breakthrough is on the other side of the difficult season you are in.

# PUNCH ONE: DIVORCE

No one goes into marriage thinking that it will end in divorce. Even if you have reservations, you still have the hope that what you are feeling is just cold feet or that love will be able to conquer it all. I always knew I wanted to be married. Many kids grow up desiring to be a doctor, fireman, musician, or teacher. I grew up with the desire to be a wife and a mother. I just knew I had so much love to give. There was never any doubt in my mind that I would be a wife and a mother. I went about my life much like playing a baseball game. First base, I worked hard on getting my college education. Second base, I focused on getting a great job and building a career. Third base, I got my degree and had a great paying job in a management position. Now I was ready for the home run, marriage, and motherhood. If only it were that easy. If only it were that simple. My life was not an easy slide into home base. I actually got knocked unconscious by a fly ball. That fly ball being divorce.

Divorce left me feeling rejected, ashamed, guilty, helpless, abandoned, angry, and depressed. Dealing with all those emotions left me exhausted. I was left trying to find my way in the world. Left trying to figure out how I had come to be in this horrible position. How was I going to survive life with this scarlet letter on my chest? How was I ever going to be pleasing to God now that I was going through a divorce? I felt robbed of my dream. I fought hard to get my spouse to work on the marriage and get counseling. But the reality is you cannot make another person stay if they want to leave. I am not placing blame. We both made our own choices, decisions, and behaviors that led to the failure of our marriage. But we all, my ex-spouse, me, and our child had to deal with the effects of the divorce.

## PUNCH TWO: DEPRESSION

As you can imagine all those feelings of rejection, shame, helplessness, abandonment, sadness, and anger led to the depression. I don't know if you have ever struggled with depression. I was in a black abyss full of quicksand. I couldn't see my way out. Every time I tried to fight my way out of the darkness I was pulled further down into the quicksand of negative emotions. I was numb. I didn't care. I wanted to give up. I cried until there were no more tears left in my tear ducts. I felt utterly defeated. I began to question my own existence. I was hopeless.

The pain was unbearable. My heart was shattered into a million pieces. The shards piercing my soul. I couldn't see how I was going to survive the pain. My saving grace was my unborn child. I just kept thinking, "How is my depression affecting my innocent child?" A child that didn't ask to be here. He doesn't deserve to be hurt by my pain. I had to figure out how to get out of this state of depression for his sake. He needed me to live so he could live. His small kicks in my womb were a reminder that I did have purpose. To be a mother. To love and raise my son.

## PUNCH THREE: STRUGGLING AS A SINGLE PARENT OF A CHILD WITH ADHD

As if dealing with a divorce and depression wasn't enough, I was also dealing with the responsibility and challenge of raising my son as a single parent. I knew at six weeks old; I had a strong-willed child. He cried for two hours, non-stop the first time I left him alone with my aunt. As soon as she placed him back in my arms, he instantly stopped crying and just looked up at me and smiled. I knew I was in for one heck of a ride as a mother. He liked having his way and could be quite defiant at times. It was hard from the start. Struggling to stand on my own two feet and care for a child with little support emotionally and financially from his father. I wanted so desperately for my child to be raised in a loving two parent home but that was not my reality.

My son's behavior issues showed up even as a toddler. The babysitter said he was defiant. It was a challenge to discipline him because he wanted his way. Once he started school, it was even more of a challenge. He was super smart, but my son could just not sit still. He was always talking in class and did not have very good social skills with the other kids. My son was expelled from kindergarten. Whose child gets expelled from kindergarten? Crazy right? But he picked up a chair and threw it. It could have seriously hurt another child. Thank God it didn't. I would get calls at work from the school literally every other day because of his behavior. It was quite embarrassing when the receptionist at work would buzz me and say, "It is the school again". They were always calling for one reason or another. Whether it was he was talking, not staying on task, not staying in his seat, being the class clown, or seeking negative attention. You name it and he probably did it.

It was shortly after being expelled, that the teacher recommended he get tested for ADD/ADHD. After the ADHD diagnosis, the health professionals recommended medication which I was totally against. But we could not get him to focus and stay on task. He was super hyper. Nothing we did seemed to help his negative behavior and hyperness. He was eventually sent to a special school for kids with behavioral issues. I eventually consented to putting him on medication. At seven years old, even he was ready to try the medication because school was just becoming too difficult for the both of us. As a single parent raising a child with behavior issues, it was exhausting. Phone calls from the school every other day, complaints from the aftercare program, dealing with his hyperness once he got home from school and trying to keep him on task with his homework. It was more than a handful. Everyone thought I just needed to discipline him more. But no one was walking in my shoes and dealing with it all. It was a lot. The emotional and mental fatigue of dealing with my divorce, then the depression, and the challenges of raising my son by myself definitely knocked me on my back and almost knocked me out!

## HOW I REMAINED RESILIENT AND THE 5 STEPS YOU CAN TAKE TO BE POWERFUL, STRONG, AND WELL IN YOUR SEASON OF CHAOS

**STEP 1: Stay Focused on Where Your Help and Strength Comes Fromz**

God never promised us life would be easy. In fact, Jesus Christ told us that we would have tough times. I had to remind myself daily in my season of chaos that God was with me in the midst of it all and He would see me through. And if He is always with us, then He will help us get through it and we will see victory on the other side. Stand powerfully on His promises. Boldly speak His promises to yourself! Seek peace by keeping your mind set on Him. Stop dwelling on the bad and find the good. Resilient people look past their troubles and put their mind on Christ. Being resilient means you never stop trusting in God even when things don't go the way you expect them to go. In the midst of the chaos and traumas of life, never give up on God and no matter what God will never give up on you.

## STEP 2: Stay in God's Word. It Will Give You Power and Strength

To be resilient you have to be strong in the Lord. You do this by reading His word for encouragement. I had to remind myself of the promises God made me. You too must stay connected to your source of strength and power. Stay in God's word so it can refresh your soul and give you strength to fight back against the struggles of life. Here are three scriptures that helped me:

☸ "Love the LORD, all you faithful followers of His! The LORD protects those who have integrity, but He pays back in full the one who acts arrogantly. Be strong and confident, all you who wait on the LORD! ~ Psalm 31:23-24

☸ "I am able to do all things through Him who strengthens me." ~ Philippians 4:13

☸ "Finally, be strong in the Lord, relying on His mighty strength. Put on the whole armor of God so that you may be able to stand firm against the Devil's strategies. For our struggle is not against human opponents, but against rulers, authorities, cosmic powers in the darkness around us, and evil spiritual forces in the heavenly realm. For this reason, take up the whole armor of God so that you may be able to take a stand whenever evil comes. And when you have done everything you could, you will be able to stand firm. Stand firm, therefore, having fastened the belt of truth around your waist, and having put on the breastplate of righteousness" ~ Ephesians 6:10-14.

## STEP 3: Pray Always

Prayer is another way you stay connected to the source, find peace, and get well again. The bible says, "Do not be anxious about anything. Instead, in every situation, through prayer and petition with thanksgiving, tell your requests to God. And the peace of God that surpasses all understanding will guard your hearts and minds in Christ Jesus. ~ Philippians 4:6-7. Prayer is how you hear from God and get wisdom and strategies on how to overcome life's struggles. I prayed that God would help me push through the chaos. I knew that fighting all that I was dealing with was going to be a slow and long journey. I needed Him to breathe life into me again because I just felt numb and listless. I prayed He would restore my hope that I would one day forgive myself and find love again. I prayed for Him to remove the shame and the guilt so I could be freed of those burdens. Remember, "Pray to me when you are in trouble! I will deliver you, and you will honor me!" ~ Psalm 50:15. God will deliver you. Never lose hope.

## Step 4: Find Meaning and Keep Pressing Forward

"We are troubled on every side, yet not distressed; we are perplexed, but not in despair; Persecuted, but not forsaken; cast down, but not destroyed." ~2 Corinthians 4:8-9. I know how hard it is to keep pressing forward but you must. Find a strong reason that motivates you to get out of bed each day and to keep fighting. I did. My reason was by son. He didn't ask to be birthed into this chaos. He didn't ask to be birthed in the midst of a divorce and my depression. He was and still is my greatest gift. I never felt like I was walking in my purpose more than when I was pregnant and being his mother.

I pressed my way through to give him the best life I could in spite of it all. It was hard, it was arduous, and I wish I could say it got easier sooner rather than later. Honestly, it didn't get easier till he graduated college. Whew Lord!! But it was ALL worth it. I am proud to say he made it through high school as a star athlete. All his teachers bragged about how bright he was. He graduated high school and went on to college. He got his associates degree in Cyber Security while working full-time. His strong work ethics and leadership skills took him from stockroom clerk to store manager of one of the leading clothing retail chains in the world. He moved into his own apartment and bought a brand-new car in 2020 at the age of 21! Don't believe them, 2020 was not all bad. I thank God that he gave me the strength and desire to keep on pressing! The bible says, "The righteous keep moving forward, and those with clean hands become stronger and stronger." ~ Job 17:9

## STEP 5: Seek Out the Lessons

James 1:2-4 says. "Consider it pure joy, my brothers, when you are involved in various trials, because you know that the testing of your faith produces endurance. But you must let endurance have its full effect, so that you may be mature and complete, lacking nothing." Trials will make you mature and complete when you learn the lessons from them. These lessons will help you to grow and do better the next time. You will become wiser and with wisdom you can navigate from an advantage point the next time life tries and knocks you down.

I learned so many lessons from my season of chaos. Here are just a few:

- ✹ I learned to forgive.

- ✹ I learned that I am never alone.

- ✹ God is with me in the midst of it all.

- ✹ Life didn't just happen to me, life was just. It was just because my decision led me into that chaos and that was ok.

- ✹ Life lessons are sometimes painful, but I can push my way through and be happy and joyful again.

- ✹ Nothing can separate me from the love of God. I no longer have to be depressed because I have hope in the love of God.

- ✹ I am a victor and not a victim.

- ✹ I learned that pain could birth something beautiful. It gave me my son and it birth my passion and purpose.

Tonya Young is a friendly, cheerful, happy, kind, and outgoing person who loves to laugh, travel, roller skate and bowl to name a few of her likes but her greatest asset is her infectious smile that can light up any dark room. She is also affectionately referred to as Mom, Gigi, Bonus Daughter, Auntie, Friend, Family, Sister and Boss lady. She prides herself in being the best role model to her beautiful daughter, Jasmine.

Tonya exudes strength, grace, unity, commitment, dedication, sacrifice and love. These attributes are but a few of many ingredients that define her as a unique individual who does not have to put limitations on life for, she believes that every experience no matter how painful or traumatic is an opportunity to learn and grow.

On a professional level, Tonya has been in the Information Technology field for over 25 years, but her passion and God given talent is in helping others. Her most rewarding accomplishments is being the owner of "An Arm Around Mom and Dad" Assisted Living Facility to provide quality care, support, and assistance to loved one's who can no longer reside independently. Also, Tonya is honored and proud to be a member of Alpha Kappa Alpha Sorority, Incorporated impacting communities and providing service to all mankind.

# Finding Strength Through A Mother's Love

I n life we always face challenges which are inevitable. Life happens with its many challenges and obstacles but ultimately, life continues even when it may seem insurmountable and may cause us to fall and remain downtrodden for a long time. But with God's grace, we can pick up the pieces of our tattered being and start the process of repairing all that seem wrecked indefinitely. I will not deny that others may not have made that transition and will never seem to rise from their adversity, but I must say that I am blessed to have faced some challenging emotional times that could have resulted in adverse and irreparable damage. Because of my overcoming these obstacles, I am grateful to share my life's story.

One tragic event ripped so much away from my life that even today, I still feel those tinges of pain as I grapple with the loss of someone so dear to my heart. I have come to accept the fact that the pain will never go away, and I have been able to take steps to heal the gaping wound left with that loss. To utterly understand what I have experienced and the deaths of its effects, let me share a glimpse of my childhood and how I grew up.

The year 1969 was a beautiful time when my parents were elated to welcome me as their second child into the world. I was the youngest of two children, my elder brother who is 5 years older than I, was born hearing impaired. I never saw him in a different light from anyone I knew. In fact, his handicap was never treated as a burden to his family and friends, or a hindrance to himself. Through conversing with him in speech, his speech developed tremendously. Conversely, my sign language skills suffered from lack of use.

Growing up, I was privileged to live in a beautiful home in a middle to upper class community where my parents ensured that we were raised properly and provided us with the comfort of rooms that were retrofitted with telephones and televisions. This was like living a fairytale as I thought of myself as a beautiful princess living in a castle. My room was just that spectacular! Furthermore, we even had an arcade room with slots, pinball machines and pool tables down in the basement. This was not only for our entertainment, but our friends also enjoyed this luxury with us from time to time. Since I excelled in my schooling, my parents also allowed me to partake in extracurricular activities such as ballet, gymnastics, roller skating, track, and cheerleading. It is fair to say, anyone would be happy with such a childhood as I had, and I credit it all to my loving family.

Every year during the summertime, I was sent on vacation in California to spend time with one of my mother's good friend's whom I call my god-mom. In 1982, there was no exception, but it felt a bit different. At that time, I remember my mom being ill and, in the hospital, unknowingly suffering from cancer. Thinking as a 13-year-old child, I thought she had a bad cold, so I did not want to leave her as I went on my trip, but I remember us arguing as she assuredly encouraged me to go and have a good time. Little did I know that would be the last time I would see my beloved mother alive. My parents must have known that those were her last days and did not want me to see her suffer. That's the summer that I received the dreaded phone call from my father stating, "Your mom has passed. I need you to come home." To this day, I still remember the words as they echo in my head, "Your mom has passed" as well as the emotional pain that I felt just knowing that I would never be able to share any more life experiences with her made me numb.

I could not understand at my young age, why the Lord would take such a wonderful, caring, loving, sweet (the list could go on and on) person away from her family and friends that loved her so dearly, especially me. I felt so lost, alone and wanted to take my own life to be with her again in Heaven. What would be the reason to continue living since my reason (my mom) was gone? I never got a chance to tell her goodbye and how much I loved her. How could she leave me like this? She was my world. Seeing my mother in her casket was the hardest thing I had to do. I grieved at the sight of my beloved mother being laid to rest, never again to be with me nor her family. This was the onset of reality where loneliness crept in. I felt truly alone with her being gone. However, I realized that my mother was in a better place with no more hurt or pain in her body so this in fact gave me some level of comfort and courage to be strong to pick up and mend the pieces and seemingly move on from the hurt and pain this tragic event has caused me to endure to be there for my father and brother. In hindsight, this may not have been the best way forward. My father should have sought some counseling for us as a family as we went through the grieving process, however, this was not done. Even in the midst of my strong mindset, I developed a fear that everyone I truly loved would leave me in one way or another. This was how psychologically damaging this loss was on my life.

But my fears were not dumbfounded, When I was around that age of 15, my father remarried. There would be no creation of a happy home as he allowed this woman to take over everything he built with my mother. This was her home and no longer the beautiful home my mother had built. Eventually, it no longer was ours as my father kicked both my brother and me out of the home, we grew up in. He chose this woman over his own children and this is when I experienced my second major loss. My dad, another person I so loved, left me all alone. I could only imagine how my mother may have turned in her grave as it would pain her heart to see him neglect his children. I remember once my mother asking me if she ever left this earth who would I want to live with and I said of course my father. I could not understand why he would choose a woman over his kids, considering how close we had gotten to each other after my mom's death. In my mind, I knew we were good children with no behavioral issues that would cause him not to want us around. We neither smoked, drink nor engaged in any illegal activities that would question the distance as he sent me off again to California to live with my god-mom to try to form new family ties.

Let me tell you that God will send you family that may not be blood. Life was challenging, and I still reeled from the pain of losing my parents one through death in the other through giving up on me. However, there are some positives to the story I can honestly remember many of the values my mother instilled in me and the lessons that she taught I thank God she taught me to aim to Excel at all times. This gave me the drive to stay focused and motivated me to continue overcoming the obstacles I faced in life. She never truly left me. When making decisions, I could see her smiling at the good ones I made and frowning at some of my terrible choices. Even though my mom was not physically with me, I always wanted her to be proud of me.

Even though God afforded me the nurturing from my family and friends who loved on me, I still yearned for the love I missed. I married at age 19 which I probably would not have made that choice being so young if my mom were still living to help guide my decisions. These are some of the decisions that I made to fill the void that was left when my mother left this earth. I do not regret these decisions because they helped me grow and I would not be the woman I am today without my story. Out of the 18 years of marriage, God gave us the best blessing any parents could hope for and that was a beautiful baby girl.

As we fast forward through the years, after my divorce, the need to be loved continued to linger and as a result, I went through three long term failed relationships. As I look back, I see where I lost myself to men, lowering my standards while upholding the boundaries I should not have. This caused me to remain in unhealthy relationships for too long that were just not meant for my life and further healing. This is what trying to make yourself whole again after you have lost a love one can do. There were times when I became so frustrated with myself As I knew that what I was doing would be detrimental to my emotional health and mental stability. How could I know what was the right thing to do but still engage in the opposite? I like the courage. For this, I berated myself constantly. You may wonder why, but no one would understand unless they have walked a mile in my shoes. Compensate for this, I dove into perfecting my motherly duties as well as my professional and spiritual life. So, in the midst of life's clouds, there is always a sun that will shine through.

With prayer and much reflection, I learned to recognize that it was okay to love me first. I used to think that loving on me was selfish but how can anyone help themselves if you cannot even help your own self. This is a selfless act. This was one of the many instances where I had to do deep meditation to try to release the effects that my mother's death had on my life. Again, I believed that if I had received the counseling in the beginning, many of the emotional struggles I endured would not have been such an uphill battle. So, professional help was sought, which included an accountability partner. This was when my healing progressed further than I thought it ever could. Also, my loving daughter helped to heal this gaping wound as she gave me such joy. It was like my mother showed back up through her with her thoughtfulness, sense of humor, and unconditional love which makes every day brighter. My mom was my biggest cheerleader then as she is today as I am my daughter's biggest fan.

Eventually, I learned how to give love as much as I desired to receive it. God has truly blessed me with so many loving family, friends, and bonus mothers that pour into me daily as I pour back into them. I am an entrepreneur as I own my own small, assisted living facility; where, as a caretaker, I get such fulfillment in taking care of others' loved ones. I can tell you that God put a purpose on my life to help others and to give the love that I so yearned for. I gratefully accept the challenges that I have and will face in life. The many ups and downs have shaped me and taught me lessons that I can pass on to other people.

This is not, however, the end of my story. I can proudly share my story and life with others as an inspiration to persevere despite the odds. Simplistically put:

- ☀ Love on your mother while she is still living. No one knows the day or time when God may call her home and leave you all alone.

- ☀ Pray without ceasing. For without God, nothing is possible.

- ☀ Even though life may pitch you a hard ball, hit the ball and run the bases because God has a home run in store for you.

- ☀ Never stop, no matter what obstacles stand in your way.

- ☀ Think about the good times shared with your loved one. The pain will never go away but remembering the light that they shined eases it.

✸ You are not alone; God is right there beside you, holding your hand.

✸ There are no options; Do whatever your heart desires and stay the course.

✸ Do not take anyone or anything for granted; If God allowed it or placed it in your life for a reason, season, or lifetime – It was for a purpose.

Realize that God has you here for a purpose. Hold your head straight and elevate yourself to rise above all adversities. No one is perfect so continue to take the necessary steps daily of being a better you. I pray that you have been inspired to hope, love, and persevere through all of life's challenges. God is not finished with us yet!

Melissa P. Latson is the CEO/Founder of MEL Developing Center, Inc. (Motivating, Elegant Ladies) a 501 c3 (non-profit) established in 2012. Her experience and entrepreneurial skills positioned her to move forward as a passionate Confidence Advisor. She sits on the Board of Directors in her community being a committed Community Advocate. Her story is her glory as a Survivor and an Advocate of Domestic Violence. Melissa teaches young ladies and women "How to Break Through the Confidence Code" in their lives in order to produce good fruit. Her desire is for all to Be the best version of who you are Becoming.

"You Determine Your Success"- Mellissa P. Latson

# Staring Through the Peephole: The Journey to Reclaiming Life after Abuse

D o you remember or have you ever watched the Lifetime Movie Channel? Often on the weekends the network would feature all real-life stories such as abuse, scandal, controlling, lies, cheating and sex. My real-life story was personally linked to these subject matters. Most women will, on average, attempt to leave an abusive relationship between five and seven times before successfully and permanently doing so. I was definitely no stranger to this statistic. He was emotionally manipulating the relationship on and off for 8 years. I didn't know what emotional abuse was until I was out of the situation. The number 8 in the Bible is considered to represent new beginnings, and a constant flow of power and energy. I was on the journey of reclaiming my life after abuse.

On the run again with my kids, leaving my own home. Going from house to house trying to escape because I knew if he would catch me, he would beat me. The time was limited to stay at a friend's house, because I didn't want to get them involved and endanger their life.

Three days after Christmas, this date is etched in my head. "Holler and I will blow your brains out" my abuser said as he snatched my keys from my hand and shoved me inside my vehicle while I was trying to enter my workplace. Fortunately, he didn't know I happened to be on the phone with a police detective who knew my current situation. Once he heard the familiar voice and our telephone conversation abruptly ended, he immediately broadcasted an alert that covered the region. We began travelling to my apartment where the events originated and began to unfold. All the thoughts of when I stared through the peephole to make sure my abuser could not harm me; those thoughts were different this time. My abuser had made it through the peephole. We were now in my apartment and he was holding me hostage. Now he was the one pacing back and forth looking through the peephole. Suddenly, he made a decision to race out of the apartment holding me tight. Officers in an unmarked car driving through spotted us fleeing to get back in the vehicle. I wanted to holler out "Help", but I remembered what he said earlier "Holler and I will blow your brains out!". Back in the vehicle we go, as we were exiting the parking lot, the unmarked car drove back around and gave the signal for us to pull out of the lot in front of them. I was a bit confused why didn't my hostage situation end at that time. They spotted me, why not rescue me? The high-speed chase had started through the District of Columbia. Running traffic lights, crashing into other cars while fleeing from the police he was driving so fast at one point that I thought the vehicle would flip over. He eluded police crossing into another county and we ended up at a stranger's apartment and there I was held hostage during a standoff with law enforcement.

Helicopters flew overhead, news reporter vans planted themselves outside, flashing lights, SWAT officers camouflaged in the woods, they swarmed the building as negotiators attempted to engage with my abuser. I couldn't believe this was my life, I thought I was going to die. Inside the building my detective friend phoned in to narrow down which apartment I was located. The time was slowly passing, I was attempting to calm down my abuser from all of the excitement that had taken place outside. I even had to do the unthinkable, have sex with my abuser at this time. It felt like I was being raped. While the T.V. was playing, a news channel reported a kidnapping at my workplace. It was about me. Is this my life? I thought in my mind. I felt like I was watching my own Lifetime Movie story, but I was still alive.

Six hours later, I was told to put on my coat and walk out the door. He said he would follow behind. I thought he was going to shoot me in the back of my head and shoot himself. Instead, he surrendered. Police flanking the door on the left immediately grabbed me and police on the right took him down and handcuffed him. Later at the police station he hollered "Melissa, I love you". Domestic violence is real as well as mental illness.

## Taking the Journey to Reclaim Power, Strength and Wellness

Even though I didn't have many bruises on the outside, they would disappear in a day or two, the bruises were planted on the inside and was meant to tear my heart into pieces forever. But GOD! When you believe, you have a But GOD moment. The nature of our God is that He redeems, resurrects and makes all things new. We are redeemed not just from something but to something in order to Love and glorify His Name. Love is a universal language, and we all want to be connected to it. Unfortunately, some are not taught how to Love. Loving yourself is first. Look in a mirror and say: I HAVE CONFIDENCE IN WHO I AM, I AM BEAUTIFUL, I AM BRILLANT, THERE IS NO OTHER WOMAN LIKE ME, I AM CAPABLE, I LOVE ME. When you don't know your worth in a relationship, abuse can sneak up on you at any given time. Relationships don't always start off abusive they begin with excitement and love like you've hit the jackpot. It's not always how a relationship starts it's how it evolves. My New Beginnings:

## New Beginning One: The Power of Faith

Often, people say there's no handbook to this thing called life. Actually, it is and it's the Word, in the beginning was the Word and the Word was God (John 1:1). Your experience doesn't change God's Word, God's Word changes your experience. As I look back on my violent experiences I encountered, I didn't think it was a way out. My Faith was very little, but when I reactivated it the healing process began. Faith in God puts you in the I AM Club. I AM filled with Faith, I AM Rich in Health and Wealth, I AM in Charge of my Life. The source of your Faith will determine the quality of your Faith. Put your Faith in God then set your eyes and mind in His Word.

## New Beginning Two: Strength from Within

Everyone has felt broken before in their own way, it's good to know your strength comes from within. I'm the type that has experienced many obstacles in my life which was meant to break me into pieces. With those pieces I put together a puzzle of who my Higher Power God says I am. Everyone is a creation of God, but not a child of God. I have access to boldness and confidence to God from within. The strength that lives in me gives me the ability to reach my highest potential.

## New Beginning Three: Life of Wellness

As I maneuver through life, I realize there's a world of ignorance to bliss when it comes to Domestic Violence. The world can be divided some will ask "Why don't she just leave" "Why do she keep going back"? It's easy to voice your opinion when you don't have a clear opinion.

It was difficult to bring my story to light, but it needed to be talked about more. I've been in a battle with myself and been debating should I or shouldn't I. Trying to block it out as if it never happened, it was like a blur. I began to think it was normal at times. Abuse is not NORMAL. My situation was kept in my home due to embarrassment and keeping family issues to ourselves. It's important not to keep abuse to yourself, find someone you can talk to that you trust. Telling my story bought me healing and healing comes from helping others. I don't want other women or men to suffer alone for years like I did. Talking about the abuse and allowing people to hear your story will give you a bigger support system. I think it is also important for people you know to be aware of the situation for your safety. When people know your history, they will be more willing to check up on you. My goal is to give a voice to women, young ladies and young girls who struggle to look in the mirror and say I LOVE YOU; YOU ARE ENOUGH. Remember, true beauty, self-worth and validation comes from within.

TO MY SURVIVORS: Hoorah!!!! You did it, you have another day to be an example to other victims.

TO MY ABUSERS: I know you've been hurt too. Hurt people, hurt people and you can get help too.

Rochelle Brightley Sherrod is a hardworking mother of three adult children. She has dedicated her life and constant focus on raising them and doting over her three grand babies.

Rochelle believes in treating others the way she wants to be treated. As a result, she has gained the respect and honor of being called "friend" by many.

Rochelle is a people person and enjoys being in the healthcare industry. Greeting people and depositing a warm smile into their lives on a daily basis is her greatest asset. She hopes that sharing her journey through this chapter will empower other women to be strong and persevere through any challenge, big or small.

# The Power of Treading Water Through the Stormy Rivers of Life

**B**etrayal Bereavement and Brokenness placed me in a very dark place in my life. So dark even that I just wanted to walk off a pier and jump in. Sitting on the very edge of that pier wondering how in the world did I get into this space. Me. The many times I blessed the souls of others through liturgical dance and I cannot save my own self. The feeling of being suffocated by the many disappointments and broken promises landed me in some dangerous rivers. Have you ever had a moment in your life when you just felt like throwing in the towel? The Meteorologist did not prepare me for what was about to take place. No bells, alerts, warnings or whistles. Nothing seems to be going right and everything went left. Drowning in despair, betrayal, depression, humiliation, bereavement and brokenness. Not finding the power to tread the stormy rivers of life.

Your mind is in constant replay of your thoughts. Your eyes are flooded with tears, you're exhausted imagining you're at the bottom of the river. Deflated. You're sinking and the images of your loved one's flash right before your eyes. Suddenly, the Anchor of the Holy Spirit grabs ahold of you, feeling a push, just enough for you to resurface on the top to breathe. Quitting or drowning is not an option! Even in the midst of the fluvial flood God still has a plan for your life!

The Power and the Anointing of the HOLY SPIRIT is real. My Truth, My Steps, My Journey, have the Power to provide others a different perspective while going through muddy waters.

Genesis 2:10-14 speaks about a river watering the garden that flows from Eden; from there it was separated into four rivers Pishon, Gihon, Tigris and the Euphrates. Each River is a representation of what I had to go through in order to reach Paradise. Could this be you?

Well tighten up that rope of hope, and say to yourself, "I refuse to sink" I did.

## THE RIVER OF PISHON (STRENGTH)

*Here lies the river of strength* and the ability to swing back from my divorce. I had to admit to myself that my marriage had come to an end and there was no way of saving a union when the *WE* spirit became an *I*. I am not placing the blame. Signing day for the divorce had finally come and to my dismay my best friend was now the witness to our divorce hearing. After the betrayal she left me feeling lost, confused and angry. The feeling of being humiliated from them both. Not only did we share everything, but she was the reason I fell back in the arms of an old love affair. I could not understand the trickery. She sold me out. We shared the same dreams as a little girl. Growing up becoming the best Spouses and Mothers we could be. Some people are scholarly driven but for me my victory dance was just getting across that damn stage. I found out the hard way that wasn't enough. My parents did not have a college degree but lived. Good living back then was getting out of the hood. I wanted my children to look up to me as their Wonder Woman. I always made do with what I had... period.

Everyone has that love of their life and for me his name was Braxton. The moment I laid eyes on him at sixteen I was hooked. We dated throughout our lives and never seemed to get what we wanted out of the relationship planted in fertile soil. Either he was in a relationship or I was, but having so much chemistry and history when we reconnected it was always electrifying. No matter what- Braxton made me feel safe. Six months into house shopping and being in a great place in my life, my credit was excellent and having some stacks in the bank made it easy to purchase a home. However, at that time it was not a buyer's market. Braxton and I thought it would be a great idea to finally pursue what we had always dreamed of. Living under the same roof. Well, I found myself taking on more roles than I anticipated. Not only was I a Mother, but became a Stepmother, Cheerleader, Nurse, Spiritual Advisor, Psychologist, Dispatcher, Banker, Loan Officer, Coach, Referee, Chef just to name a few from the University of Life. Even though we managed to walk through all the seasons of life yours mine and ours, it did not work out in our favor. Although I never doubted the love, he had for me, it just wasn't enough to keep us grounded. Way too many hip huggers, naysayers and relatives who kept the stew brewing. Many thorns in a bush. One in which swung by every weekend bringing droplets of poison to the fold then returning to her safe haven. Promises were made but not fulfilled. A lot of withdrawals from savings and no deposits. Words of comfort, "Babe, as long as I am good you good. I will never hurt you again". I came to the table with a pretty package. Left many nights crying myself to sleep wondering what my next move will be. Tyler Perry's movie "*Acrimony*" finished up my love story with Braxton. I could have played the part my damn self.

Ending the relationship with Braxton was indeed one of the hardest meaningful things I had to do. My character, integrity and Legacy was on the line. I was not going to ruin my Legacy based upon someone else's frivolous behaviors. Worked too damn hard building. Losing not only a mate but a best friend felt horrible. You say stop playing the victim I say I was the victim. The deception and feeling of humiliation, being robbed, double-dealing, pain and resentment bruised me very deeply. I fought really hard wanting to hang in there and make things work but found myself waiting for what I wanted from him as he continued with his life even though he kept promising that we would be together. For the betterment of oneself it was time Braxton packed up his feelings and kept it moving. The stinging wound of anger and resentment just manifested as my soul of strength exited my body into the river stream.

# THE RIVER OF GIHON (BURSTING FORTH)

*Here lies the river of the ability to keep it moving.* I had to bottle up those feelings I was feeling inside and do just that keep it moving. I still had two children to raise. Working three twelve hours shifts during the week to make ends meet Queen Mother had to make it happen.

Even seeing their Mother deflated with brokenness I still had to be a Mom. I prayed often.

Read scriptures. I never stopped church services and found myself listening to podcasts before COVID-19. My Dad's illness had taken a toll on him. Just when the healing process for me was gearing up, here comes a Tsunami.

For you see, Dad was diagnosed with Vascular Dementia some time ago and was getting worse. Some nights after work I had to help Mom carry my Dad upstairs to his bed. I gave him baths and continued taking him to his appointments. My Dad was not one with a lot of words but his presence was so peaceful. I reassured him I would never leave his side. He was so scared.

It hurt my soul seeing him this way. I refuse to cry in front of him. I don't know what's worse, watching someone pass from an illness or dying instantly. My opinion the pain is the same. This routine office visit wasn't so routine. My Dad's Neurologist told me at this visit that we were at the phase of his illness to just love him up at this point. He was given weeks to live.

My focus then shifted solely on my Dad. Living thirty minutes away from my parents the wear and tear was killing me. I had to be strong for my children, my nieces and my grandchildren. The family decided on bringing hospice into the home. Dad was a very private Military Man. My family worked around the clock to keep Dad comfortable. My nights now consisted of tossing and turning because I had to take care of my Dad, but I did not want to pack this stuff up yet again. This cannot be happening, not right now. Oh my God, my poor children. They do not deserve this. After much prayer and given the direction to move, the holy spirit told me to pack it up and enjoy the rest of the days Dad had left on this earth. I did just that and did not care what anyone thought. Dad passed away just three months later and watching his transition from earth to glory was something to see. We gathered around his bedside singing praises and oldie but goodies. I wanted to switch places with him. He cried. We cried, but gave him the feeling that we will be okay, just go and rest. Whew, was I overwhelmed. My God! My Dad was my Everything!! My children made sure their Mom was okay under the circumstances. The homegoing celebration for my Dad was exactly what he desired without flowers, because he hated flowers. I cried and my tears flowed like a river. The feeling of emptiness. I lost the only person who protected me. My soul cried of a different loss; a loss of grief exited my body in the stream. This time my Dad followed.

# THE RIVER OF TIGRIS (GOD HURRY UP)

Once the dust settled, I finally took the liberty in taking the invitation to an outdoor football fantasy event. Dallas and the Redskins were playing and I was super excited to take part in watching my Dallas Cowboys beat the Redskins. Listen, I am having the time of my life when suddenly...I felt sluggish and the need to lay down for a quick second. Not familiar with my surroundings I fought back the fight to rest my eyes for a bit. All I remember was waking up in the back of an ambulance hearing the sound of the alarms. Oh my God, am I having an out of body experience? What the hell is happening? I began to pray. Where are my kids?

*Here lies the river of immediate attention from GOD.* **I Need you now Lord.**

The EMT asked me all kinds of questions I could not answer because I could not talk. I can't even feel my arms or my legs, am I paralyzed? What the hell? Patiently waiting for my children to arrive at the Emergency room watching the unsettling urgency of the ER Nurse staff and Doctors in and out lifting my arms and legs to see if I had control of my limbs. NO stability at all. My only form of communication was crying. My daughter finally arrived who happens to be a Registered Nurse, BSN, gave me the comfort that I needed. The Doctor had just informed my daughter that her Mother is having a stroke. A stroke? Dear God. What? My baby boy slid down the wall with the bad news screaming come on Mom you can beat this, you're a strong woman, as the tears rolled down my eyes. Even in my worst condition I did not want to hurt them for they have been through enough. I am supposed to be their Wonder Woman. my nieces, my daughter in law, were all crying at my bedside. They tried very hard to be strong, but it was just too heavy. Firstborn son holding my hand gently placing my cellphone by my side, listening to the melodies of Yolanda Adams sing my song, "The battle is not yours it's the Lord's". I played this song every morning as we headed to First Christian Community Church of Annapolis. I heard them tell my children that they were going to administer the TPA. But they had to move quickly. This medication is a tissue plasminogen activator for a quicker recovery. Everyone's body reacts differently toward the medication, so the first twenty-four hours are critical. You're placed in ICU to be monitored. No sleep, they check on you every 5 minutes. Some people have multiple strokes and pass away. Others overcome with the abilities to recover. I was one of the lucky ones. God has a plan for my LIFE and I thank GOD for it every day and take nothing for granted. Watching my children and my nieces go through the process of wondering if I was going to live will forever play in my mind. God once again answered my prayers and healed my body. This really was an eye opener and told me that I was not okay and if I did not make some changes it may not be the same next time. It scared me to death. I was only forty-eight years of age and allowed myself to get all worked up over things planted in my wagon that I did not place there. I had to come up with an action plan. I had to throw the lifesaver around my own damn neck to save me. Now I treaded the Rivers of Pishon, I dived into Gihon and backstroked into Tigris. I could no longer please everyone.

# THE EUPHRATES RIVER (FRUITFULNESS)

So, I listened to the Holy Spirit and my children's advice and relocated to another state to rebuild my Being. I declared that I am taking back everything the Devil stole from me. For I knew I had one more river to cross and in order to enjoy the ambiance of this river, work had to be done. *For here lies the river of Paradise.* This river was Orchidaceous. I had to learn how to love myself all over again. I had to forgive myself for giving away my power. I had to forgive those who hurt me and took my kindness for granted. I had to Forgive myself for being who I needed to be at that time. Yes! It's a work in progress every day. Say NO! No one will ever love you the way you loved them It's a gift and a curse so stop looking for it. Learn to adhere to your gut feelings and discernment. It never fails you: Even though I tread the Stormy Rivers looking back I am enjoying My Peace. My New Creation. My Becoming. Time waits for no one. So, when it feels like you cannot hold your head above water, just remember, there is a life preserver by the name of Jesus who will save and help you swim your way through trials and tribulations. You got this!

**Read the Word (meditate)**
**Do not fall prey while healing**
**Encourage Yourself-You can do it.**
**Listen to podcasts**
**Mind says:** *You know we've failed before, right?*
**Heart:** *And we're allowed to start again*
**Soul:** *And Again if we need to*
**Your Anchor awaits you!**

Lakisha McGaney-Osei, HHC is an author, speaker, and the Founder/CEO of Joy is Just Over Yonder, LLC and holistic health coach who provides health and wellness experiences through collaborating with other health coaches, mental health professionals and other wellness gurus. Her signature experience, Wrapped in Wellness, premiered in 2019 and continues to be a sought-after platform to gather even in the virtual space. She is the Lead Reflexologist and owner of I Touch Soles and heads the Journey2Amazing movement.

Coach Lakisha has been inducted into the Legacy Holistic Health Institute's inaugural Health Coach Hall of Fame and is a proud 2019 graduate of the institute. She holds a B.S. in Kinesiology from the University of Minnesota, and has a passion for coaching and guiding women to Live, Move and Overcome, on their Journey2Amazing. You can contact her at hello@joyisjustoveryonder.com. Follow her on FB @journey2amazing and @joyisjustoveryonder.

# From Dwell to Well: How I Drilled My Way to Wellness

There she is. Know that she will be a Victor. She is strong and vulnerable. She is embracing the Queen unconditionally and without limitation. The scars are there to remind you how far you have come. She operates in her overflow now. Her well runs deep. She is Power. She is Strength. She is Well(ness).

> *"You don't want to lose too much weight girl,*
> *your head will look big."*
>
> *"We are big boned honey, you got it honest."*
>
> *"You better slow down, you look like you on that stuff."*

All my life I had to fight...and I know this is not The Color Purple, but the sentiment is relevant. All my life I have witnessed my aunts, cousins and myself battle weight. It has been an unending fight for some of us. I, and over 42.4% Americans, are considered "overweight or morbidly obese." Though these are based on European standards, there is no denying that we have an obsession in this country with unhealthy foods, many as a result of the fast-paced rat race that many of us have to partake in daily. We simply are led to believe that we do not have the time to prepare healthier choices. Unfortunately, we do not always make the healthiest choices and sometimes we normalized the bad choices in your circle of influence. What do I mean by that? We emulate what we see and model our lives after that or make a very definitive decision that that is not what I want and do the opposite. For instance, it was very normal at our family gatherings to partake in massive amounts of sugar through eating several cakes and pies as if it was almost a competition.

*"Oh she nice and thick."*

*"Look at that booty."*

*"Don't nobody want all that stomach."*

Growing up, I remember being 9 years old and in Mrs. G. Smith's 4th grade class. Early on I had already shown myself to be quite athletic and was typically the captain on the playground or one of the first to be picked because of my speed and strength. This year is etched into my head almost 40 years later because it was the year that I really began to discover the likes and dislikes of my body as it began to change almost overnight. At 9 years old, I had already begun developing a pretty sizable chest and was a 32 or 34 C by the end of fourth grade. This was also the year that I biologically "became" a woman. Yes, old Mary came to visit me and my mom explained what was happening and showed me how to clean up and use these thick napkins to put between my legs. I was so proud the next day to go to school and tell Mrs. G. Smith that "I will probably need to go to the bathroom more than usual the next few days since you know, I have my menstrual." Yes, that's how I said it. So here I am at 9 years old quite developed, and with my menstrual flowing. It would be years later that I realized the correlation between weight and the onset of your cycle. My menarche was two years earlier than the average age of 11-14 years old for the first menstrual cycle. According to a study by Science Daily, there is a biological trigger that happens when you hit around 100 lbs (2010). Your body is recognizing that if you were to carry a child, it would be able to support the development of the fetus and the carrier. This makes sense when you think of gymnasts who are well into their teens before they begin their cycles due to their low body fat. Because I was so athletic being bigger seemed to be a plus. As my body continued to fill out and I became more involved in basketball throughout middle and high school, I realized that playing sports was my way to keep things in check. https://pubmed.ncbi.nlm.nih.gov/4053451/

What happens when we no longer have that natural way to keep things in check? For years I knew even if I picked up a few pounds in the off season, I was going to get that frame back in shape once conditioning started for basketball. This was true throughout high school and college. In college I was at one point so obsessed with being lean that I could not wait to take a caliper test that we had to do in weight conditioning class. Calipers measure the mass between two points. There are also electrical readings that send electricity through you to determine your body mass. Everyone was amazed when it was my turn to do our electrical BMI reading that my body fat came back at 9%. I mean I was a lean machine! Though I do not see myself pursuing that number now, it is a reminder that I did that! I was running regularly back then and had a very fast metabolism. Why am I telling you all of this? Because many of us can relate to the moment we began to see our bodies differently. You can relate to how you embraced or didn't embrace those changes based on how they were explained to you or not explained. Our bodies begin to take on a life of their own and that can become scary.

Our bodies hold history. Our wombs hold history. Our hearts hold history. As women we go through stages, we experience being in the prime of our lives, we experience forgoing ourselves to take care of others, we experience the need to reclaim our bodies, mind and spirit. Much of how we experience the reclaim is based on what we experienced growing up.

So now what? I am not 16, 25 or 30 anymore. How do I reclaim my life, my peace? How do I refill my well? Know that it doesn't happen overnight. Remember me, 9% body fat, 160 lean lbs.? I remember being young and saying I will never go over 200 pounds. But what I was really saying to myself was I never wanted to get to the point where I could no longer move like I wanted to move. Where I couldn't comfortably walk upstairs without losing my breath. However, after birthing 3 children, marriage, several moves, separation, back together, separation, graduations, job loss, job gains, and all the things life throws at you, I creeped over that 200 mark with my first pregnancy and never looked back. Before I knew it 200 became 220, 220 became 250, and 250, became 280. So, my new goal became ensuring I would never hit 300 lbs, absolutely not! For me, there was that threshold that I ensured myself I would never reach, no matter what, but crept up on me while I was living life. For many of us who are mothers, daily routines begin to not include time for yourself and you just have enough energy to satisfy the household while you remain spent and worn out. You are serving up the best of you to the church, the organizations, the job, the family, and when you look down at your own plate, you realize you have forgotten to serve yourself. Your well, has run dry. You don't have anything else to pour out, and ain't nobody pouring into you.

The first thing you have to realize is that it is not all about numbers only, it is about the levels as well, i.e., blood pressure, resting heart rate, etc. Yes, some of us may want to weigh a certain amount, but we also have to know and understand that there are so many parts to your well that need attention. What can you do to create an overflow in your life again? How do we protect our health and wellness in an environment where we as women are always expected to give? I did several things to begin reversing the drought I was experiencing. I would like to share with you some of the steps that you can take to Be well. It simply includes being intentional about where you DRILL your Well.

Dig Ditches dig/dig/ break up and move earth with a tool or machine, or with hands, paws, snout, etc.

My personal journey with my weight fluctuating is a rollercoaster that I have been on for years, but now I have made the decision to not look back. Somewhere along this journey I took a detour and stopped digging ditches for me. Digging required me to break up and off some things that no longer served me and to begin plunging deep into those things that are beneficial in my journey2amazing. I began to dig ditches of time. I block out time daily that is for me, even if it is only 15 minutes, where I can not be bothered. Over this past year I was intentional about digging out time for trekking (walking and hiking) in nature solo and with small groups of friends. It is crucial that you create this guilt free time for yourself. There is power in being willing to dig as many ditches as you deem necessary to create your foundation for complete wellness.

*"When a well "runs dry" it doesn't mean*
*that the well will never produce water again." - Unknown*

Resolve the Residue res·i·due /ˈrezəˌd(y)oō/ a small amount of something that remains after the main part has gone or been taken or used.

As I began to drill my well, I realized there was some residue that was still left from experiences over the years that led to me repeating the same cycles. I would go through periods of working out, focusing on changing what I eat, see results and then for some reason fall back into that dry well I was trying to dig myself out of. An experience that was very beneficial to me resolving the residue was taking a 6-week womb healing course. It was very therapeutic and allowed me to dig deeper into my well and resolve some issues that I didn't even know I was still harboring. This journey2amazing calls for your therapeutic well to be filled as well. You get to decide what that is and know there is no shame or embarrassment in seeking out therapy.

Impact vs Impress im·pact /ˈimˌpakt/ have a strong effect on someone or something.

As I focused on drilling deep in my own well, the ripple effect has led to a residual impact on those around me. It is far more important to create impact than to focus on impressing those around me. Folks can be impressed with you in the moment but take no action. But when you create impact it motivates them to take the information and apply it to their own life. I am here to impact you, not impress you. I began a squatting2amazing journey that I started documenting to hold myself accountable. It began as a one-month journey and now we are on a mission to squat for 100 days straight. I don't do it to impress others, but doing it has certainly impacted others. You never know who is watching you, but be certain that someone is.

> *"The only limit to your impact is your imagination and commitment." Tony Robbins*

Live Full Out live[1] /liv/Remain alive

Yes, it seems so simple and matter of fact. But I had to choose to live full out. To not simply exist and fulfill my mundane routine but to allow myself to start checking off my adventure list. Why wait until death is near to start living? In 2019, I committed to going or doing something amazingly different every quarter. That included going to Ghana, taking my first cruise, spending a long weekend in Vegas and hosting my first sold out Wrapped in Wellness event to close out the year. It was an invigorating year. And those trips were a God send as each one kept my spirits high between several family members passing away. It was like God knew that I was going to need some refuge. Allow some spontaneity into your life. It sure does a body good. Even in the times of Covid-19 you can be very strategic about planning safely.

Learn for a Lifetime learn /lɜrn/ gain or acquire knowledge of or skill in (something) by study, experience, or being taught.

It was also very important for me to re-educate myself so I dug a ditch of self-development that included an year-long holistic health coaching program. I found this to be more life changing than my college degrees. It is never too late to learn a new skill, a new hobby, a new activity that will keep you moving and meeting new friends. I found a wonderful tribe in the health and wellness space because of my connection to my classmates and the founder of Legacy Holistic Health Institute. I went on to get certified in Reflexology and Level I Reiki. The possibilities are endless when you are open to learning for a lifetime.

Drill sis drill! Your well shall overflow as long as you keep:

*Digging Ditches*

*Resolve the Residue*

*Impact vs Impress*

*Live Full Out*

*Learn for a Lifetime*

Here I am. I am Victor. I am strong and vulnerable. I am embracing the Queen within conditionally and without limitation. The scars are there to remind me how far I have come despite the droughts and residue and how deep my well runs. I am Power. I am Strength. I am Well(ness).

I want to leave you with 5 Affirmations to manifest your Power, Strength, and Wellness.

*I am taking back my Power:*

*1. There is Power in Digging Ditches..*

*2. There is Power in my Residue.*

*I am Exuding my Strength*

*There is strength in my impact.*

*I am Prioritizing my Wellness*

*There is healing in Living full out.*

*There is healing in Learning for a lifetime*

Grateful and blessed to say that Dr. Emma Neal is the Founder and CEO of Empowerment and Life Coaching Services (https://www:empowermentlifecoachingservices.com). I have over 20 years' experience in Healthcare Leadership and Clinical Operations. Authored Women Leaders Experiences and Perceptions regarding under Representation in Health Care Administration. Education consists of a Doctorate in Healthcare Administration (DHA), Master's in Health Care Administration (BSHA), Associate in Medical Assisting Technology (AAS),

Medical Claims and Billing Specialist (MCBS), and Nursing Assistant (NA). Also, a certified Master Life Coach of advanced training in life purpose, happiness, goal attainment, and coaching methodologies. A member of the National Society of Leadership and Success.

I pray that the testimony of my life inspires you to know you have the strength, the power, and wellness in achieving your life goals. My aim remains to empower as many women as possible in achieving their goals. Allowing your self-esteem to stand in the way will only be holding you back. I would like to thank God for the many blessing to continue this powerful journey with my daughter in a new book in 2022.

Thank you to Delayna Watkins for this new opportunity to be a co-author in SHE IS WELL.

# Creating Harmony While Working Multiple Jobs

A small-town girl from West Virginia (WV) sixteen and pregnant. It was not exactly the vision I had in mind. I had been dreaming of going to a University living in a dormitory while at the same time enjoying life with my friends. My life had been one of turmoil and I knew it. I was angry as well as a single mother unsure of what to do next. What was I to do now? Get a job or receive assistance from the state? These were the questions I kept asking myself repeatedly. I had always been on the honor roll and never missed a day of school. Now, I would need to learn how to balance my life, a baby, and maintain a job or two to survive in this town I called home.

A WV free article (2013) stated, "teen pregnancy often poses real challenges to young women and the ability to stay in school and earn a living wage; it places a burden on the parents of the teen mother and father; and it often locks families and communities into a cycle of poverty, joblessness, and dependency on state assistance". This chapter will include my personal experience growing up in West Virginia as well as caring for a baby, the stresses of my life, and achieving a balance between maintaining multiple jobs.

Living off the minimum wage in West Virginia, I realized I was nonetheless in trouble. My mom and dad did not have a lot, even though they did the best that they could. I had been adding to their financial stress. My little girl was my whole life and I loved her unconditionally. My life remained a complete mess at the age of nineteen working at two fast-food places. I did not have the confidence or the ability to control my actions or make good judgments at that point. I had a baby right now, so whatever was I thinking of to fight on the job. I find myself standing in the dining room trying to explain to one police officer my side of the story. A place that I realized I did not fit, because there was racial discrimination at its finest. I had been facing discrimination as well as have lived it in this small town.

The white supervisor put all the blame on me. I was the only African American employed at that moment. Realizing I could be in trouble with the law. This would have left me without a job to provide support to my daughter. Whatever bit of confidence I had disappeared right through the door. I was feeling weak and frightened while my emotions were all around the place. I did not want to tell anyone about this, even my mother and father. The shame and guilt of fighting the white lady tore me down. I was not raised in this manner. I was telling myself that she initiated the fight and then let me end it. That was not the right mindset to have. This young girl was supposed to be away at college not trying to defend herself to the police officer.

My feelings overtook every single muscle in my body. The first thing I could imagine then was that I am about to go to jail. Tears and sweat began pouring down my face. All because I was asking for help at a time when the supervisor was laughing and playing in the back-kitchen area. I had taken pride in my work and never missed a day. I can remember a white couple in their mid 60's eating in the dining area approached the officer. I had been instructed to step aside by the police officer while this couple provided their side of the story. Twenty-minutes seemed as if it were a lifetime.

My self-esteem happened to be at the lowest level not knowing the outcome. To my benefit, the local police officer comes up to me saying I am free of charge and could return to work. The husband and wife had told the truth expressing the entire incident was not my fault. What I didn't realize was that the man was quite well established within the community and ha a considerable amount of money and authority! I had been asked by the police officer if I would like to press charges against the supervisor. I said, "by no means" and asked if I could just go home.

At that point, I realized I had plenty of thinking to make regarding my life. Working two jobs however not for certain regarding my life and how to control my income. As quickly as the paycheck arrived the cash had disappeared. I enjoyed going shopping, partying, and eating out. Trying to pay the rent, childcare, as well as my bills became overwhelming. However, the same couple stumbled across me one-year later while at the same time praying for me and my daughter's strength. At that moment I knew changes needed to be made. They had faith in me when I did not. They brought me beneath their wings getting me registered to attend college in my hometown. They paid for my initial year of school to get me started.

At that point, my mother and father nor I did not own a vehicle, therefore I was forced to walk to work, school, and my daughter's daycare. I can remember my dad walking with me to pick my daughter up at the daycare center in the snow. It was so cold; I could hardly feel my feet. That did not prevent me from pursuing my goals. I received my one-year nursing assistant diploma and my associate in medical assisting technology. Determined and committed not to let my little girl down, I felt like I owed her so much. I went ahead with school and received a bachelor's degree. My daughter was my motivation.

Life appeared to be moving in the right direction I thought. Fast-forward into my early 20's my entire life was going to change yet again. I met the love of my life a gentleman that loved and cared for me deeply. The following two years of dating I asked if he would take my hand in the marriage. To my surprise, he said yes. Twenty-four years later we are still happily married. I realize a few women would probably have not done anything like this, however, I wanted to get married. My husband and I have had our fair share of sleepless nights, money issues, and health issues, you name it we experienced it. My husband has been a great father to my daughter.

Therefore, my dreams were to have another baby with my husband. This is when the chronic pain and the bleeding began. I stayed weak and hardly could move for months. My physician diagnosed me with multiple tumors. I had to have emergency surgery to remove the tumors along with one of my ovaries. My possibilities of becoming pregnant were not looking great. After that nightmare, I have been offered two jobs at two different healthcare facilities in leadership. I accepted both positions. A few years passed and the chronic pain and bleeding started back again. Was I was losing my mind? What was going on in my body? This was so stressful starting my new jobs and now this again.

Fast-forward to my late twenties the tumors were growing back yet again this time over thirteen. I was devastated. New husband, a daughter, health issues what a mess. The physician had given me the news of my life, as well as the decision I made, was nothing except faith. I became pregnant despite having multiple tumors. The doctors felt with the tumors growing that my baby may have deformities and did not recommend me keeping it. I decided to carry my child and take that risk. I was considered high risk during my 9 months of pregnancy. The first two months were very stressful because of all the scar tissue from my first surgery. Doctors had a hard time seeing the fetus. I had about 4 sonograms before the doctors finally had great news my baby was not in my tubes. Immediately after the birth of my baby, physicians indicated I would require surgery again. Nineteen years later I have a healthy baby boy. Not one tumor touched my son. Yes, a miracle child. I am at peace with God, so I was okay. I have two wonderful children and a stepdaughter that means the world to me. My life was back too normal.

I made a promise to myself to take care of my health, my family, and maintain my three jobs.

My husband supports me only because this is something I want to do. I continue to work full-time in 2020. Forty-plus hours a week in healthcare leadership and clinical operations, part-time as a supervisor in retail in the evenings, and two weekends a month sixteen hours shifts at a very prominent healthcare facility. I understand this is a lot and some people would call me crazy. For example, in a six-month time frame, I have earned enough income to live happily and start my new business. I realized that various sources of revenue would put us where we need to be. I refused to live paycheck to paycheck anymore. Not to tell anybody up until now writing this story about my real life. The importance of balancing work and life you will still need to take some time out for your family and yourself.

When you touch the heart of your children you know you have done your job as a mother. This is a perfect example from my daughter Starbrille Cooper:

My mother Dr. Emma Neal had me at the young age of 16 years old. However, she did not allow her having a child so young to get in the way of her success. For as long as I can remember my mother has always worked extremely hard. She has never been a lazy person at all. My mother has done everything she could do to make sure she could provide for herself and her daughter. I remember going to my mother's college graduation when I was 5 or 6. Growing up I remember my mother working a full-time job at a doctor's office later going to the hospital at night to work. She would always come to my track meets to support me.

As I grew older, she continued her education and never stopped. I went to her master's degree commencement ceremony. It was such an amazing experience. There are no other women I know on this earth that works as hard as my mother. Not only is she a hard worker, but she excels at anything she touches. She wrote a book and published it after she completed her doctorate. Which is an amazing accomplishment. My mother leads by example and she supports my dreams and goals. Sometimes I have no idea how she does everything. Working full-time, two part-time jobs, and starting her own business. She does so much, and she is still able to spend time with her family.

There is no doubt in my mind that one day my mother will be a world known speaker, author, and entrepreneur. Anyone who meets her sees the same thing I see an amazing woman. I love my mother so much and I am proud to be her daughter. There are so many things I have learned from her and still learn from her every day. My mother is a woman who has worked for everything she has set her mind to. She took having a daughter at a young age and became a successful woman for her daughter to look up to. Thank you Star for your wonderful words."

## Takeaways and tips for balancing and maintaining multiple jobs:

Sharing my story is extremely important to me to inspire other women not to ever give up.

1. Taking good care of the mind and the body is the most important thing to reduce stress and burnout when trying to maintain and balance multiple jobs.

   A. Some important factors are exercising regularly, such as yoga, walking, and weightlifting. This is an extremely important part of my self-care

   B. Spa treatments once or twice a month

   C. Drinking plenty of water

   D. Rest on your off days

   E. Try to eliminate eating unhealthy foods and sugar

   F. Finding a good mentor or life coach is a benefit to help move you forward

   G. Save the best for the last- vacation is very important

I give my loving husband most of the credit for always supporting my dreams and helping me find myself when I was lost and stressed out. While earning my master's degree and doctorate I continued working my jobs. Without God, none of this would be possible. I had to be strong-minded and make some major decisions about my life. I was hungry for more and the need to share my story with other women. Do not give up on life or your goals. All things are possible if you just give it a chance. I had to do a lot of praying to get to where I am at today.

## Reference:

WV FREE Report on Teen Pregnancy and Childbearing, (2013).

https://www.wvperinatal.org/wp- *content/uploads/2014/09/WV-FREE-Teen-Pregnancy-Research-Report-Issued-June-2013.pdf*

Quentoria "Que" Leeks, was born and raised in Georgia. Her greatest and most important role is being a mother to her three amazing sons. She is a Preschool Director for the City of Rockville. Que's dedication, hard work, and determination to avoid a life of poverty and mediocrity inspired her to go back to school to earn her degree in Early Childhood Education. She is Strong, Resilient, Ambitious, Adventurous and a Survivor. She is an inspiring Author.

Que has been in the early childhood field for 15 years. She is a real-life example of beauty for ashes. She was the first Drive to Thrive award winner in the Single Parent Achiever Program and after 4 years of hard work, growth and dedication she is now nominated as 5th Single Parent Achiever of the year!

Que hopes that sharing her story of overcoming and climbing a mountain of obstacles will inspire other women to find the strength and support to push through and keep going.

# Rose Amongst Thorns: Blooming in Difficult Situations

## Thorns:

Life for me hasn't always been easy or even pretty, I was born to a drug addict and an alcoholic. But I am building from a foundation that is solid and equipped for challenges. At the age of two years old I was sexually molested by my mother's boyfriend at the time. When I was 4 years old, my mother walked out of the house going to the store and she never came back. The neighbor called the police because she hadn't seen my mother in a while, and I was taken to foster care. I went to a group home and then was placed with a foster care family for about 8 months. The day before my 6th birthday my grandma came and got my sister and I out of foster care. My Grandma lived in Albany Georgia, which is 3 hours outside of Atlanta where I was born and was being raised. Oh, how nice, right? Well, she only wanted us for a check, that's what living there felt like. I was verbally and emotionally abused (Verbal abuse and emotional abuse are often used interchangeably, but while they might overlap, they are two different forms of abuse with distinct characteristics). I stayed with my grandmother until I was 13 years old then she sent me back to Atlanta to stay with my father while he was living in a motel. Being a parent at a very young age may really affect and destroy your future. I have been a mother to someone since I was 13 years old. Becoming pregnant at a young age I experienced a wide range of emotions, from being shocked, depressed and disappointed to constantly worrying about my future. Not only did I feel all those emotions, I also felt guilty as I became pregnant because I was sexually violated. I felt guilty because in my mind I allowed myself to get raped by putting myself in the vulnerable situation. I was living in a motel with my dad back then and I went with my friend to a party in another room at the hotel where there were older men and they gave us dark colored drinks which must've had something in it because before I passed out, I remember one of the men laying me down and taking my clothes off and my friend wasn't anywhere to be found. The next thing I remember is waking up in my room in the wrong bed with my pants down. Now I didn't know I was pregnant right away. I had move back with my grandma and my PE coach pulled me to the side and was like, "baby you picked up weight are you pregnant"? Me in all my 13-year-old sense said, "no I'm not I've been living in a hotel and we ate a lot of fast food". Needless to say, she called my Grandma and I was taken to my primary care doctor and he confirmed that I was pregnant. That was in February and my son was born in May. You know what was worse than being raped was nobody asking or even caring enough to ask you how this happened and making up lies. I was told I wasn't "fucking" right because if I was, I would have never gotten pregnant. I lost friends I even had a cousin on my dad's side father tell her she couldn't hang out with me because I was a bad influence. I was pulled out of school and finished the 8th grade home-schooled where a teacher dropped off packets for me to complete. I spent most of my days alone. I would like to think that's where my self-isolating comes from. A month after I had my son my Grandma put me on a bus, and I ended up back in Atlanta at the bus station with all my stuff in plastic bags and a baby in tow. By the grace of God my dad was a cab driver and he eventually pulled up to the bus station and collected me and my son. He had no clue or idea I was coming back to Atlanta as a matter of fact no adult knew I was on a bus with a 1-month-old baby. My dad was still living in a hotel at the time he eventually got a duplex we lived there for a couple months before my dad ended up getting arrested for fighting. I was sent back to Albany to live with my Grandma because I was still under her custody. At this time my Grandma was living with her husband and he did not want me living in his house, so during the day I would go to school from there, but I couldn't sleep there. I would sleep at one of his daughter's house on the floor in her living room. That lasted for a few months until I had an accident where I was on my period and I didn't have a change of clothes to change into, so I just laid there in my bloody clothes and she got mad at me. During this time my Guardian Angel, my son's godmother was helping me with my so since he was born. I met her when I was eight years-old she was a home health nurse that came into our house. She would get my son on her days off and bring him back when she was going back to work. When my son was 10 months old my grandmother told me, I should let her get full time custody of my son so that I can finish school because education has always been very important to me and I was going to school during the day and up all night with a crying baby. My son's godmother agreed to keep him under the following conditions: that I didn't have another baby and that I finish my education she kept him from 10 months old until he was in the third grade. Shortly after she gain custody of my son I was sent back to Atlanta.

## Planted:

I was able to complete High School and graduated top 10% of my class while living in a hotel with my dad! I was also able to attend Fisk University in Nashville, Tennessee. My time in college was amazing I established a relationship with Christ and found Him as my Lord and Savior. When I regained custody of my son, we moved into an apartment I got a full-time job and was unable to finish school as it became too much to be a mom, work and go to school. Eventually, my bills became too much and upon facing eviction I moved back home to Georgia. While living in Georgia I had a friend from college who had recently moved to Maryland because she had transferred schools. She invited me to come live with her because she was approved for a two-bedroom apartment and didn't have a roommate, so I sold my car to rent a U-Haul, packed all of our stuff in it and my son and I drove to Silver Spring, Maryland. We stayed with my friend for a few months before she asked me to leave and now, I was miles away from family and only had a few friends from church but we were basically homeless. The church pastor let me store my things at their home office and my son and I went into a shelter program where we stayed in different hotels that the state would pay for when they had the funds.

# Blooming:

After almost a year I was able to get my own place. Never thought I would have another child, but I had two more boys and fell into a deep depression as one of my sons has some developmental delays and was having trouble staying in daycare which affected my employment and my ability to provide for my family. His future became my focus. While trying to get my son the services he needed I also had to take some time and get myself the help I needed to get past just surviving as I always felt there had to be more to my life then just barely making it and having to choose between needs because I didn't have enough to cover everything. In the words of Maya Angelou "My mission in life is not merely to survive, but to thrive; and to do so with some passion, some compassion, some humor, and some style." To create a decent future for myself and my succeeding generations, I invested in myself by forgiving myself for past mistakes and forgiving the past, not forgetting but truly forgiving people who didn't even apologize I had to recognize that everyone did the best they can in their given circumstances. If they knew better, they would have done better. I started seeing a therapist which was a hard task as I was so closed off and didn't want to deal with anything but going to therapy has provided me a space to learn, grow, and heal. Therapy has been effective for helping painful experiences become tolerable. Another thing that has help me get beyond survival mode and into thriving is having an awesome support system, a power circle of people who see me properly, they didn't see me where I was at but they saw the potential on my life and they poured into me and loved me even when I didn't love myself. My power circle gives me a support system I wholeheartedly and truly believe in. My power circle makes me better. My power circle includes biological, created and church family. My sister and her kids moved to Maryland providing the type of meaningful support from biological family. I learned to trust others by learning to trust myself, and by opening my heart I was able to have flourishing relationships, see the opportunities around me, and begin to live a more fulfilled life. You can choose your friends, but you can't choose your family,' so that boring old saying goes. Well, I'm calling bullsh*t. We can choose our family too. My created family are people I've known for years and they are very essential to my growth. My church family is one of the greatest blessings in my life. They are my safe place. The church family that I belong to greets me with a smile, hugs me, and asks me how I'm doing…and really means it. I have a wonderful group of people who are brothers and sisters in Christ who care for me and love me deeply in a myriad of ways. I joined Single parent Achievers, a support group for single parents which has improved my quality of life and made me more Intentional with my parenting. I also won a "Drive to Thrive" award and I'm being honored as the Single Parent Achiever of the year for the Class of 2020! I was able to go back to school and get a scholarship, I'm eight classes away from obtaining my degree, I have a reliable, part-time, steady job for which I am paid enough to support myself and my family without it being a struggle, and I became the Director of the preschool program which was one of my career goals. There was plenty wrong with my life but there was also a lot right. But I learned that I AM A SURVIVOR, I am no longer just coasting through life!!! There was a time where I was stressed, worried and couldn't afford to take one more hit, I struggled from low self-esteem and lacked confidence in myself and my abilities. I was Surviving at the bare minimum. Today I am no longer isolating, I'm walking in happiness, I'm truly joyful and enjoying my life as a mother, sister, and a friend. When the test and trials come, they are no longer wiping me out they are little bumps in my road. I'm owning who I am and being unapologetic about who I am. My needs and wants are covered, my life is flourishing. My "why" for healing, is so my kids will have a childhood they don't have to recover from. Pressure and stress create beautiful things. Diamonds withstand incredible pressure during their creation. The clam deals with the annoying piece of sand during the creation of a pearl. The caterpillar deals with the stress and pressure of creating and being wrapped in a cocoon and having to break free before finding freedom in a new form. I have had a lot of moments that feel like MY PERFECT PLAN…fails. And my Plan A, turns to Plan B…and then Plan C…and then Plan D…and sometimes all the way down to the letter Z. In order to bloom where you are planted you must; 1. LOVE WHO YOU ARE RIGHT NOW… know that you ARE enough. 2. FIND YOUR WHY: God has put you where you are for a reason – so find that reason and BE that reason. 3. DON'T QUIT: Keep walking. Keep trying. Pick yourself up and go again and again and again. It's my hope that you learn to bloom where you are planted. Even if you find yourself planted under some concrete at the moment, look for the crack in the concrete to find your way out.

LeTysha Montgomery is a jewelry designer, entrepreneur, empowerment speaker, international and best-selling author, endometriosis advocate & podcast host.

Stand Out Style specializes in one-of-a-kind beaded jewelry in various styles & colors. I have sold my creations in retail stores & small businesses, showcased to a national chain buyer in Los Angeles, & been interviewed by at television station in Lawrence, KS. I have received several blue ribbons (Maker of Merit) & have been nominated for Top Accessory Designer of the Year.

I am a national empowerment speaker whose topic is advocating for your health & yourself.

Amazon Best Selling Co-Author for the book Women Inspiring Nations: Volume 3 I'm Still Standing.

Podcast host for Endometriosis: Journey to Butterfly. A podcast about my journey with endometriosis that was created to educate & raise awareness about endometriosis!

https://podcasts.apple.com/us/podcast/endometriosis-journey-to-butterfly/id1473744089?uo=4

https://standoutstylejewelry.square.site/

# Embracing Self Advocacy as an Endo-Warrior

Imagine living with what you were told were "normal" period symptoms-painful cramps and a heavy flow that make you want to stay in bed. Every woman has those issues is what you are told, but do they? Does every woman have severe cramps that start when they first get their period? Personally, I have had severe cramps ever since I started my period at 12 and a half years old. Are these normal period symptoms? I have been told for over 25 years that these are normal period symptoms. But I don't know if I truly believe that.

Most women don't talk about their periods to each other, let alone complain about these problems to their doctor. When you do talk about these issues with your doctor then you seem to be told that you need medication aka birth control pills or an IUD. Now that sounds like an agreeable solution, but do we truly know what the problem is? Most of the time they don't offer an explanation or reasoning for your issues. Or are we just masking the symptoms and pain to keep the patient happy and out of the office? Technically, when you are on some sort of birth control you have fake periods or sometimes no period at all. So, the thought is if you don't have a period then you won't have painful cramps. Maybe you will or maybe you won't. I was on birth control in June of 2019 when I went to the Emergency Room.

Are we truly searching for answers to help or just providing temporary solutions? I have had so many ultrasounds in the last 15 to 16 years it's crazy. Of course, they never find anything. I have had transvaginal ultrasounds as well. I have had CT scans as well only because I have repeatedly complained about my pain. These test show nothing unusual so therefore they stop looking and just try to push medication more or a different type.

What if everything you have been told actually wasn't normal? I can't tell you how many times I heard that some women just have more painful periods. Some have cramps, heavy periods and etc because it's normal. Yes, some women do have painful periods because they have a disease or another medical issue causing it. What if there was a reason or an actual cause for the pain? Imagine if there was a clinical diagnosis for the reason you had pain. It was actually a disease and no you won't making it up.

Maybe a visit to the right Ob-Gyn doctor fifteen years ago would change things. After explaining my symptoms and giving timelines, the doctor gave endometriosis as a possible cause for my issue. In my head I am thinking, endo what? Like what does that even mean. What is that? I had never heard that word in my life and little did I know that day, that word would be used again later in my journey. Nor did I know the word endometriosis would change my life forever. Unfortunately, it took 14 years from the first time I heard that word for me to official be diagnosed.

Endometriosis is a word that has been used off and on in my journey over the years. Unfortunately, the person who has used the word the most is me. I wanted to find out everything that I could about it. What causes it? Honestly, they still don't know what causes it. Is it genetic? Possibly there could be a genetic link.

Is it fatal? I found that no, the disease itself isn't fatal. But there can be complications depending on where else it is besides the Fallopian tubes, ovaries and uterus. Also, it depends on how bad your endometriosis is. Is there a cure? There is no official cure. Again, depending on where your endometriosis has spread to even getting a hysterectomy may not get all of it.

So many questions, but so few answers. One thing I found out thanks to the pamphlet given to me by my doctor is a laparoscopy is the only way to diagnosis it. So, you have to have a surgical procedure to verify endometriosis. How many diseases require surgery just to get a diagnosis? That seems totally crazy to me, especially given all the advancements in medicine that we have.

## Clinical Definition of Endometriosis:

Endometriosis (en-doe-me-tree-O-sis) is an often-painful disorder in which tissue similar to the tissue that normally lines the inside of your uterus — the endometrium — grows outside your uterus. Endometriosis most commonly involves your ovaries, fallopian tubes, and the tissue lining your pelvis. Information came from mayoclinic.com.

Laparoscopy (from Ancient Greek λαπάρα (lapara), meaning 'flank, side', and σκοπέω (skopeo), meaning 'to see') is an operation performed in the abdomen or pelvis using small incisions (usually 0.5–1.5 cm) with the aid of a camera. The laparoscope aids diagnosis or therapeutic interventions with a few small cuts in the abdomen. Information came from Wikipedia.

Endometriosis affects 1 in 10 women or anyone with female anatomy.

Fast forward to June 2019, the month that would change my life forever. I have a better tolerance for pain, but the second week of June in 2019 was my breaking point. See, I thought I could struggle through the right ovary pain like I had for the last two weeks. But that night before I went to get checked out, the pain was way more intense. I seriously thought my ovary was going to burst, or I was going to die of extreme pain. So, I gave in and went to the Emergency Room, which wasted about 4 hours of my life. That visit also resulted in a horrible visit with the Ob-Gyn doctor they recommended a few days later. I knew that I had to take matters into my own hands and call my own Ob-Gyn.

So, I called, and of course, I would have to wait until August. August seemed like a lifetime away (two months) and my pain had gotten no better. I was assertive and told the scheduler I needed a sooner appointment because I was in severe pain. It was at that moment; I became an advocate for myself and my health. I didn't realize that being an advocate would change my life. By advocating for myself, I got a sooner appointment on July 8th. But this visit would be unlike any other that I ever had. Before that appointment, I knew what needed to be done. I made the decision that I needed to have the laparoscopy to see if I had endometriosis. I had exhausted all my other options (ie: tests and medications) and surgery was all that was left. So, on that day I actually agreed to a laparoscopy to see if I had endometriosis. The doctor probably felt like it was her decision, but it actually was my decision.

Never in my wildest dream did I think having surgery would be my idea. But I knew my body and that it was crying out for help. That Emergency Room visit was a wake-up call to advocate for myself because I know my body best. Surgery was scheduled approximately a month later in August 2019. I was so scared about the surgery but knew it needed to be done. I read all I could about endometriosis and the surgery. I even watched YouTube videos about the surgery and packed an overnight bag like instructed. Even though it's an outpatient procedure there is still a chance that you might need to be admitted overnight for observation.

I had no idea what I was in for, but was headed full steam ahead. I remember asking all of my friends to pray for me. I remember one of my friends who works in the medical field was very help and informative. They told me what foods to eat post-op, what types of things to pack in my bag, and even what types of clothes work best. I had never had surgery like this before, so that information was so important.

Surgery day was here, and I was in a pretty good mood. I was finally ready to face my fears. I wanted to feel better and get an official diagnosis. Was I nervous? Most definitely, but I didn't let it stop me from what I needed to do. I can't explain it exactly, but I came out of the operating room a different person than I was. I had a higher pain tolerance, was more in tune with my body, and had the belief that I could handle anything. I was a new person in some aspects. Surgery went fantastic, my recovery went well, and I took no pain medication post-op after being released.

In September 2019, I finally was diagnosed with endometriosis. It was a bittersweet day filled with many emotions. It was good to finally know the diagnosis, but the details of the condition were still unknown. Endometriosis doesn't have a cure, and medication can help some people's pain. I really didn't want to be on medication. I was tired of the pill and just wanted to listen to my body. Honestly, the pill just masks your symptoms so you forget about them. I am an endo warrior and don't want to mask my symptoms.

Endometriosis is like a roller coaster because some days are good (no flares) and some days are bad. On the good days you go out and get things done. And on the not so good days, if need be you rest. There will be days when you question yourself and wonder how you ended up being the 1 in 10 that have this. On those hard days find comfort because you are strong and so is your body.

I have to admit that I had a false sense of security after my surgery that things with my endometriosis would magically be better. In some aspects that was true and in others it wasn't. I thought 2019 was a bad endometriosis year, but it was nothing compared to 2020.

Endometriosis really took me through a struggle in 2020 another ER visit, messed up my cycles 9 out of 12 months, ruined my 40th birthday and had me travel to see an endometriosis specialist. These things were taken well except ruining my 40th birthday in which I wanted to go out of town.

In 2020 my body was still adjusting to life post birth control pill, post-op, and it just took me all over the place. Which made me understand why some women get off birth control pills only to get back on it. Yes, it makes my period easier, but what is it doing to my body. My cycle was a nightmare some months, but I survived and am doing what's best for my body.

Life with endometriosis can be hard, but we are warriors who can't let this disease stop us! Yes, there will be days you are miserable and can't do anything. But hopefully those days are far and in between. My hard days teach me the most they are what make me track and try to find a correlation between my symptoms and foods on various dates, plus advocate for myself. Those hard days are why I do the things I do to bring awareness to this disease. Hard days make you and give you your warrior power.

I feel like my endometriosis journey has been going on forever and has been split in two parts - before the diagnosis and after the diagnosis. My journey before the diagnosis was long, but my journey after the diagnosis is harder. Having a diagnosis is a significant change, but it also makes it more difficult to get the help you need, especially if you don't want medication or a hysterectomy.

The most important thing endometriosis taught me is to advocate for myself. No one else is looking out for my best interest but me. Advocating for yourself is so important, especially for your health because you only have one body. You don't realize how strong your body is or how much it goes through until something happens. Speak up for yourself and your health! Don't be afraid to switch doctors, get a second opinion, or even ask for other options. You know your body better than anyone else. You will never regret advocating for yourself and your health!

I learned that I am stronger than any pain. Pain is a way of your body letting you know that everything is not okay. The longer you ignore the pain, the worse it will get. Try to push through the pain to find the root cause of the pain. Personally, I feel that sometimes different medication is used to mask the symptoms and the pain. If you aren't having any pain, then you can't complain about it. Do what's best for you and your health. In terms of my endometriosis, I have decided to treat it holistically and naturally as I can, except for surgery, of course.

Also, everything happens in its own time and own way. Everyone's journey is unique. My endometriosis journey took over 14 years to get an official diagnosis. They say the average is 8 to 10 years. That is a big difference in terms of 4 to 6 years earlier that I could have been diagnosed.

The different options and decisions that could have been made both personally and professionally doing that time. Endometriosis affects every aspect of your life!

We don't always understand why things happen the way that they do. If I would have had the surgery any other time besides when I did, I wouldn't be doing what I am now.

I am teaching others about endometriosis and advocating for themselves and their health. I feel like my health journey wasn't just for me, but it was for me to educate and share with others. I use my journey as a testament to others. Hopefully, it will inspire others to push through the hard days and not to give up on getting help. I share my story so hopefully others don't have to go through what I went through in terms of having to wait 14 years for a diagnosis. And, to let other endometriosis warriors know that they are not alone in their journey.

Endometriosis is a disease that isn't going away and doesn't have a cure. So, it's something that needs to be discussed as much as possible. I feel like education is the key. I am thankful for my journey in order to use my voice to spread awareness. I have learned that sometimes having surgery can led to bigger things than a diagnosis.

I hope this story inspires you to find out more about endometriosis. If you are an endo warrior, know that you are not alone and keep pushing. If you know someone dealing with endometriosis, be an ally to them and let them know you are there if they need a friend. Let them know that they are not alone. Most of all understand that endometriosis affects everyone differently and we all have good and bad days. Just offer us understanding and grace when we have to cancel plans or don't feel well. Trust me, it's not an easy decision to make and we all feel we are superheroes!

Superhero steps to advocate for yourself. I challenge you to use them!

**1.** Speak Up
You know your body better than anyone else. Don't be afraid to speak up and advocate for yourself- it might save your life.

**2.** Documentation
Write down your symptoms and the dates. See if there is a pattern and go over the details with your doctor.

**3.** Don't be afraid to get a second opinion
You know whether or not your doctor is taking your concerns seriously or not. Sometimes it takes a new perspective or a fresh set of eyes and ears to help you.

**4.** Don't Give Up
Take the time be persistent and never give up on yourself or your health

Always trust your journey and yourself!!

Here are some amazing endometriosis organizations as well:

https://www.endoblack.org/

https://www.endofound.org

Welcome, I am Afrikus Hart, your experienced, certified Nurse. I am here to help you walk in your confidence again. I understand what it's like to feel insecure about how you look in your clothes, self-conscious about how it fits and not wanting to take pictures. I know how hard it is to lose and maintain your weight as I struggled with my own weight since childhood. I had gastric bypass surgery in 2012 at my highest weight, which was 320lbs. Now I have maintained around 172lbs. I created Confident Bodies and Wholeness as a full-service holistic spa center. I offer you the support, services, tools, and resources you need to get the body you desire without plastic surgery! I understand the confidence you gain by small victories like being able to fit into that outfit or to finally be able to get your dream outfit on! For me, it was a jumpsuit. Now I love the camera, can't you tell! No, I'm not perfect but I love how I look, and I love the new me! I am walking in my confidence and you can too! Read my chapter to learn how...

# Walking in My Confidence

*"Learning to love myself was one of the hardest
things I've ever done."*

When I was younger, I was molested by someone close to me that caused some residual effects in my adult life such as my actions, feelings, how I react or overact to situations and most prominent is my difficultly with trusting people in my life. For years, the trauma from my childhood manifested itself in many ways such as self-doubt, comparison, anxiety, overthinking, guilt, resentment, and seeking validation from people who could barely uplift or encourage themselves.

*"Comparison is the greatest thief of joy."*

Do you feel like you are not enough? Like everything has to be perfect? Why are they doing better than you are? I know how it is to let self-doubt and comparison consume you. I can be the biggest cheerleader for someone else, but when it came to myself, I had very little confidence. Doubt would often creep around in my mind. I started to question my skills and abilities. I suffered from the imposter syndrome for a long time. I felt like I had to achieve an abundance of accomplishments to feel worthy.

Did you take a lot of training just to prove that you could? Some of the classes were irrelevant, some were useful for my career, but they were done to prove a point—that I am good enough. I frequently doubted myself, even with all my knowledge, education, and skills. I would always have an agitated feeling like I need more, when I have everything I need to succeed in my everyday life.

I cannot compare my journey to anyone else's because what God has for me is for me. I must be patient and know that it will come in His time, not mine. That I AM enough, I AM worthy. I AM confident. I AM capable. I AM great. I would often observe, what appeared to be an outpouring of blessing on others. With a humble heart, I wondered, why them, not me? What makes someone else worthy of such blessings, while my life feels like it is in despair? Then, I would have to realize that I do not know another person's journey or struggles. What may appear to be blessings, could just be that—an appearance, a show, an act. It was time I realized; I cannot compare myself to others. I needed to focus on me, my goals, my endeavors and my successes, no matter how miniscule they may seem to anyone else. As a nurse, I would doubt myself in my own profession, as I thought my field is oversaturated, but everyone brings a unique talent to the profession. I bring something to my brand and my business that no one else can. I used to feel competitive, but now I realize that you get more from collaborations. There is enough for everyone.

*"Do not compare your life to others. There's no comparison between the sun and the moon, they shine when it's their time."*

Do you ever feel anxious? Raises both hands. Yes, that's me, too. People who suffer from anxiety often have intense, excessive, persistent worry and fear about everyday situations. This is how anxiety presents in my life. Some people may not have noticed that when I am anxious, I ramble—a constant need to talk to someone. I usually do not have a real topic; I just have a dire need to engage in conversation via in person or lengthy telephone conversations. However, there have been times that I have been able to identify my feelings and was able to tell someone I was experiencing anxiety. I felt empowered to be able to finally verbalize my feelings. If I knew what was going on and was able to tell someone else, then I felt empowered.

For me to keep feeling important when I did not have anyone to talk about, I would take more classes than I needed to just so I can check off another achievement. I did this, simply for self-gratification. At the time, I did not care if I hurt someone's feelings or shared private information as long as I was in the spotlight. Now I really see how that damaged relationships because then I was known as a busy body gossiper who talked too much. They could not see that I was hiding from pain, that it was a defense mechanism. Can I blame people for not wanting to confide in me anymore? Nope. I tried to escape those four dreaded words—"we need to talk." By the time any conversation occurred between and adversary and me, I had at least ten different scenarios in my head that I have played out what you're going to say, how I responded and about four possible endings.

*"Cast all your anxiety on Him because He cares for you." 1 Peter 5:7*

*"Repent and turn back so your sins can be forgiven." Acts 3:19*

God is not keeping score of your failures, faults or shortcomings. He said as long as you come to Him confess your sins and repent then you will be forgiven. Have you ever done something you are ashamed of, something one would think is unforgivable, feel like you are not worthy of happiness? There are some things that I have done in my past that I am not proud of and because of my actions. I felt like I was not supposed to be happy. How could I be happy, I should not be because in my mind I did not deserve the it. It was not until I truly began to pray to ask God to forgive my sins and to release the guilt from those sins. I was so sure that there was no way that God would forgive me so, I believed that anything bad that happened to me I deserved because it was karma for my past sins. After I began to pray, repent for my sins, and prayed to release the guilt, I started to feel some of that weight lifted. I began to feel love. I began to feel worthy. I began to feel stronger. I began to feel forgiven. I felt like I was enough. No one is perfect, we all fall short in some way or another. I had to focus my prayer on being able to forgive and remember without feeling. To this day, this is one of my prayers. It helps me to accept things that I cannot change and not to hold on to anger and resentment. Have peace.

*"If we confess our sins, he is faithful and just and will forgive us our sins and purify us from all unrighteousness." 1 John 1:19*

I had to learn to love me and know that I am wonderfully made in God's image. I was always trying to seek validation from others and let my anxiety take over. Through my growing pains, some of my friends did not like to talk to me because I would go on and on and on. They did not know that my anxiety was a defense mechanism, that when I became nervous, talking was a method to calm my anxiety. I would ramble or talk about things to try to make myself feel important. I would talk and gossip about others and had to know the latest hot topics. I needed to feel important and included. I was the social butterfly being included in most outings and get-togethers. I would be extremely hurt if I was not invited or knew about what was going on in the family or in the community. Then I had to learn that I am not going to be included in everything. I wanted to be included, as exclusion made me feel like a failure and failure was never an option.

Because I was dishonored as a child, I felt like I always had to know what was going on. This was a method I used to protect myself or prevent something bad from happening. I made sure I was well aware of my surrounding and the people around me. I exactly what was going on at all times and this gave me the power to be in control of a situation. In later year, I have come to realized that everything is not meant for me to know. I know that people are entitled to their privacy and what is shared with me should not be shared with everyone else unless given permission to do so. I would take things personally if I got into an argument or if someone said something negative about me. I was always in defense mode, explaining mode or outspoken mode. Although, I do not like confrontation, I had no problem speaking my mind.

Looking back on things, my main issue was that I suffered from anxiety. That is how my body and mind dealt with my trauma. In addition, anxiety can manifest itself is by: overthinking. excessive worry, second guessing, mind reading, worry about past events, uncertainty, controlling behaviors, and over planning.

*"Be anxious for nothing, but in everything by prayer and supplication, with thanksgiving, let your requests be made known to God; 7 and the peace of God, which surpasses all understanding, will guard your hearts and minds through Christ Jesus."*
*Philippians 4:6-8*

*"Therefore, if anyone is in Christ, he is a new creation. The old has passed away; behold, the new has come." 2 Corinthians 5:17*

You have to heal from past hurts in order to move forward. You have to forgive. I have always been taught forgiveness if for you, not the other person, therefore, you proceed in life carrying a baggage of hurt and pain. I was a negative talker and thinker because it was hard for me to see the good in people that pain is powerful. Seeking therapy or counseling services in the black community is taboo and often not talked about. I highly disagree. For me to heal, I sought a spiritual healer. She allowed me the platform to release my feelings in a safe environment. That in itself is therapeutic. I was able to talk about my feelings, release that hurt and know that what happened to me as a child, was not my fault. I was finally able to let go of that weight. I cannot control what someone else did that they have to own their actions; I cannot take on that responsibility for them. That is a time where validation is important, for someone to acknowledge your pain and validate that it was not your fault it is more freeing than you can possibly imagine. I wanted to be loved and feel worthy so I would overcompensate for almost everything. What I needed was to love myself and look in the mirror for self-validation. However, I felt unworthy to be loved because I still carried the guilt of things that I had done wrong in my past. In my mind, I did not deserve anything. I would question everything. I was raised in church and believed that Jesus died for my sins but I thought, how can he forgive me for what I have done? How can I be worthy of anything good?

Currently, I stayed prayed up all the time. I read my scriptures daily. Any issue that I have, I talk to God about. I have a little talk with Jesus, I tell Him about my troubles and I leave it to Him. He is my refuge and my place of safety. He is my God and I trust Him. For so long I was trying to seek validation from other people, as they say looking for love in the wrong places. I needed to turn to God. He is the only one who can give me peace, to allow me to see me like He does. He is able to forgive, to be able to let go of the past, to heal my inner child. He is the only one who can help you see your worth and value. When you go to Him, go with an open heart and cast all your worries on Him and let him do the rest. Let go and let God.

I pray every day, several times a day. If I get stuck, not sure what to do, feel myself starting to worry......I pray. I thank God as soon as I take a breath in the morning. I thank Him for waking me allowing me to see another day. I thank Him for his continued protection and traveling mercies throughout my day. Some of my daily prayers are to: help my unbelief & increase my faith, to forgive and remember without feeling, to be more of service to others, to release the guilt of my past sins, to allow me to forgive myself, to be humbler, to change my heart, to release the overthinking, release the self-doubt, release the self-sabotage, release any negativity. Daily affirmations are a great way to instill positivity into your day. I recite daily affirmations to encourage myself or to give me an extra boost. Some that I say are: I am enough. I am worthy. I am loved. I am confident. I am uniquely me. I am grateful to add value. I have all that I need. I have the power to control my thoughts. I am at peace with my past. I choose to be happy. I will not compare, compete or covet what no one has. My time is coming.

My process was not easy and neither will yours, but it will be very much worth it. You will have to put in the work to get the results and healing that you need and seek. Also remember, you have years and/or decades of hurt. It is not going to be healed overnight. There will be days where you are going to wonder, 'why so much pain.' I now see that I need to let His will be done if it is meant to be then it should have to be forced, it should come naturally. In my professional life, I do not have to know or understand everything. In nursing school, everyone has to learn how to learn in nursing school you have to know why, why this is happening so you can figure out how to treat it and in life. As medical professional, we do not always know why. I now know that I do not have to be included in everything, we all have different types of relationships, and that I do not need to keep trying to force things to happen. It will happen in His time, for His will. When you are hurt by a man you can tend to forget your Heavenly Father's love for you and how to have a peace that surpasses all understanding. I walk in my confidence of who I am, loving who I am and knowing that I am uniquely me.

Carleeka Basnight-Menendez is an author, award winning life coach, and a prolific speaker with global appeal. As one highly sought out for her innovative approach to wide-ranging topics, Carleeka has earned both, a domestic and international respect from the world stage.

She is the creator of the F-IT Method, The A.V.E., and Menopause and Mimosas; offering new and aspiring Christian female entrepreneurs, the skillsets needed to increase visibility, earn a solid income, and impact the world from the dimension of their purpose.

Her coaching and consulting brand is one of a kind, as Carleeka offers consultation, strategies, and direction for clients looking to reform their lives.

Carleeka believes that when you change your perspective, you are then able to change your life. She takes clients from being sick, silent, and stuck, to creating the lives that they demand; with no compromise.

# Becoming A Whole Woman

I am thankful I am not where I used to be, can I get an Amen! Girlfriend my life has had ups and downs, challenges and my faith shaken but I cannot give up or give in because I am still becoming the woman God has called me to be. I am writing this to encourage you that you are still being made even in the midst of disappointments, discouragements and being discontented. When I was 22 years old, I was this vibrant, smart college student with BIG goals and dreams of becoming a doctor, a surgeon to be exact. I was focused and determined to not let anything or anyone, including me stop me from achieving my goal. Sounds good right, of course it does. How many goals have we set and did not obtain due to life and circumstances or situations? It was my junior year at my favorite HBCU Norfolk State University, when I was sitting in Biology class and I had to get up and literally run to the bathroom. I got to the restroom and started vomiting.

This went on a few times out of the day, and I was thinking that I just had a stomach bug. Well, as the weeks went by this feeling did not subside. It got worse. Now, I was still having my monthly cycle so pregnancy was not on my mind. Now, I did not say that I wasn't having sex but I could not be prego! Some of my friends were like ohhh you are pregnant, so one night while at a friend's house I took a test and y'all when I saw those 2 lines I could have passed out. All running in my head was OMG how am I going to tell my parents. Let me backup just a little. I forgot to mention that I am a PK (Preacher's Kid). I called the father, who is now my husband and told him. Fast forward I finally told my Mom and we went to the doctor. Thinking that I am only a few weeks along or so, but I was actually almost 5 months, not showing just sick. I remember sitting in the doctor's office embarrassed, shameful and disappointed in myself.

Honestly, the only thing I remember him saying was that I needed to gain 50 pounds. Huh, what, who? Me, the 80-pound young woman who had a fear of getting fat now was being forced to gain weight. I cried like a baby. I was battling so much internally along with people and their snickering and talking about me externally. I continued to go to church when I was not in the hospital or on bed rest. I began to feel like I was lost and a huge disappointment to my family. There was so much weighing on me that I kept bottled up inside and it was killing me.

Quick run-down, a man who is on deployment while I was pregnant, eating disorder, my family not approving of him and of course church people, and people wondered why I was so sick. I would cry myself to sleep so many nights wishing a few times that God would not allow me to wake up. The words of me being fast and man-ish would play in my head often. That's why we have to be careful of what we allow people to label us as and what we say and think about ourselves. Although, I was attending church after being sat down from the things I did, I would look around at others that I knew were doing the same thing or sinning as well and they were still up serving and what not. I have never been one to throw someone else under the bus, but I knew it was not right.

People laughing and smiling in my face and then talking about me wasn't right, but I said, "you did it to yourself". Don't get me wrong they were talking even before that. LOL. Nevertheless, while I was sat down from my church duties until after I had the baby, there was no restoration. I did not have anyone check to see how I was doing mentally. To pray with me, share scriptures of encouragement, etc. Thank God I made it through, but with no conversations and prayers of restoration I had my daughter and two years later I had my son. I already knew what was going to happen and I did not feel like I did the first time around. Look, don't judge me, but before we decided to get married, I was pregnant yet again with my third child. So, I jokingly say I did it for the father, son and the holy ghost!

My sin was the sex before marriage not my children, and God allowed it to come to pass, because years later at the age of thirty I had a full hysterectomy. That surgery changed my life forever in so many ways. I felt like I was less than a woman and the mental struggle was real. I had no guidance or support. Other women did not talk about their experience. Who could I talk to about what I was feeling and going through? No one, so I bottled it up for years until I started talking about it more and opened the conversation for other women as well. What if I never opened up and was transparent?

Look, we don't choose what we go through, but we can choose to open up our mouths and share our journey of struggles and successes with someone else and know that God has a plan for your life and there is nothing that can stop his plan. Through my experience of having my children out of wedlock I understand how shame and guilt can weigh you down. You may be feeling like you are not worthy and that your life has no meaning, but that is a LIE from hell! Even in our poor decisions, mistakes and disobedience God still loves us. During this time in my life, I was still being molded and becoming the woman God wanted me to be.

The thing is this is just one aspect of me becoming more wiser, stronger, anointed and resilient. It didn't happen overnight, but it took prayer and practical steps to get to the next level. I had to move myself and believe that I was more than my situation. I had to change my perspective about me, not what others thought, felt or said. If I would have remained broken then I would still be sick, silent and stuck trying to please and live for other people. When are you going to let it go and GO? Girl your time is now and only you can stop you.

We all have a story that needs to be heard, to build and encourage someone else. I know that I was not the first young lady nor the last, but someone needs to know that their life is worth living and their children are a blessing. In this process I am determined to speak out because there was more to me than just this situation. I could have allowed myself to self-sabotage the next place in my life, but God. The term becoming is merely the process until you get to the other side. Every day I am becoming a better version of myself and you should too.

Every day that we have breath in our bodies we have a chance to love, forgive and do something different to make a difference in our lives and someone else's. The choice is yours, so what will you choose to do? I have made up in my mind to keep evolving, learn the lessons needed in my failures and disappointments and I want you to do the same. Girlfriends keep becoming the woman you're supposed to be, because another woman is waiting on you to walk it out, so she can do the same. Three things that keep me going in spite of what I may face is my faith, being able to face the challenges presented to me and being committed to fulfilling my purpose. Our faith will be tested but in those moments it's a stretching season to pull something out and to allow God to work in you. Take time to elevate and ignite your faith. Give yourself some grace while facing the obstacle(s). Many times, we give others so much grace and so many chances, but what about you.

No matter what you have done, forgive yourself and keep becoming. Lastly, decide that you are going to be committed to the process whatever that looks like, What I went through then I eventually grew through. I have not arrived, but I am continuously growing, evolving and becoming a whole woman emotionally, spiritually, physically, financially in every area of my life. You are not on this journey alone and even if you lose a few people during your evolution it's ok, you better keep going!

Angela B. Sanders is known in the community as Ms. Health Concierge and has been working in her passion of nursing for over 3 decades. Her career has span to touch the lives of others in the areas of the Hospital setting, Hospice, Long Term Care, Home Health, Research and Community Activist as she encourages self-care and personal wellness.

Angela holds certifications for Nursing Assistant Training Educator, Hospice Liaison and Legal Nurse Consultant. Her most valued focus is on Health Education in the communities. She is the creator of **Man Up Wise Up** and **Suited for WELLness** which are programs designed to help Men change the mindset of how they view their Health to gain a Healthy Living Lifestyle through mind, body and spirit that will last for a lifetime

Angela is known for her contagious positive spirit, her enthusiasm for others well-being and her passion to deliver and engage her patients and clients in their health journey. She educates and encourages them to participate in reversing their thinking to promote a healthy journey for a lifetime. Building a legacy for them and their families is what matters!

Angela in her spare time enjoys traveling across the world, listening to music, being an entrepreneur, visiting her family and networking throughout the nation. Her health motto is #Health is #Wealth. It is the most valuable asset you will ever own!!!

Angela lives by the scripture of **3 John 1:2** Beloved, I pray that you prosper in ALL things and BE in health, just as your SOUL prospers!!!

Angela can be reached at mshealthconcierge@gmail.com

# From Divorce to Divine Interception

I dreamt of a house in the country with a yard full of trees, Magnolia to be specific and two children, a boy and girl to raise with my high school sweetheart the man who had vowed to love me and be with me until death do us part. I was so happy to be his wife. No other person next to my Dad had significant meaning to me than this "man" who had swooned me off my feet, dated me without judgement and gave me gifts the size of his heart. Based on our thriving relationship I would have an amazing life together, forever so I thought.

## THE SiN

Music filled the air as we cruised down the highway. I was singing, bopping my head to the music on the radio and popping my fingers as if I was that girl. How ironic that Aretha Franklin's song *RESPECT* was playing on the radio. He was driving in silence. I could see his lips moving as he controlled the wheel. I thought he was singing along with the music as well. He kept looking at me with his lips moving. So eventually I turned the volume down on the radio so I could hear what he was saying. At that very moment as the volume went silent, I heard the words, "I'm GAY." It hit me like a ton of bricks. I sat there paralyzed with my mind spinning like a revolving door. My facial expression froze, my eyes revert and my heart skip beats as I gasp for air. Everything just kept spinning. My hand clutching my chest is when I awaken from this nightmare. My alarm clock goes off. I jump up in a panic looking around as if I was in an unfamiliar place. I start to relax so I could catch my breath. I sit in bewilderment trying to process this nightmare. My mind just constantly spinning trying to interpret what just happened. Had I been so naïve to have not noticed that something was wrong in my marriage?

Weeks go by and gray areas start to appear. My thoughts are interrupted as the mailman knocks at the door. A letter in a baby blue envelope had come from our car insurance company. I preceded to open the letter and I begin reading it. Our truck had been involved in an accident which I had no recollection of. It stated the driver, Mr... (not my husband's name) and my mind goes blank. I think about the nightmare that is now confirmation that GOD was removing my blinders so I could see! How long had "this" been going on? I sit down and my body goes limp as I began to sob an ugly cry still holding onto the letter. The thought of 26 years kept ringing in my mind like a revolving door. The noise grew louder and my emotions ran wild from anger to insanity and back to anger like a vicious cyclone trying to land in a barren place. How dare he vacate these premises without notice! I have lived my life with the title of Mrs. and HE is just gonna take it away like "I" meant nothing to HIM at all. You never gave me a chance to voice my concerns about this marriage.

# GOD's Plan

I remembered the women who played major roles in my life growing up down south. Their strength of how they overcame obstacles in their life was a sounding board for me to draw my strength upon. You have "it" in you to do this. In the midst of my head spinning "I" heard a whisper…BE still and know that I am GOD. Your exit will be a masterpiece creatively designed for you and the plans that I have for you. You will lack nothing. Jesus, give me the strength to do this! With every fiber in me I moved from that spot that had supported my lifeless frame. As time went by, I continued my normal routine as best as I could. I begin to form my exit strategy. My thoughts were interrupted. The phone rings and the representative asked to speak to the lady of the house. The representative initiates the identity process to ensure I am the right person. He says, "as of next month we will begin the foreclosure process". Holding the phone in my hand was all I could do. My mind drifted like waves in the ocean. Envisioning ways to destroy his life like he had destroyed mine. You said, "until death do us part." Well, it's coming up. You are going to replace me and my position with some dam "balls?" Who dah F?CK do you think I am, in my (Beyoncé) voice!!! When your husband, your best friend, your protector interrupts 26 years of marriage without any consideration in how it affects you, disregarding your feelings and not validating the "SiN" he has created all you want is instant revenge by any means necessary. This is the "ultimate betrayal." The saddest part about betrayal is it *never* comes from your enemies. I have every right to take his life. Come back to earth Angie! He ain't worth it. Ok sir, with my voice cracking, I will call you back on Friday and make a payment.

I check the mailbox. Envelopes from…Baltimore Gas and Electric, water bill and All State car insurance were all past due. I just sat there trying to figure out how am I going to do this? Leave my home of ten years, leave my memories. How will "I" explain to my young adult children we have to move because their mother can't afford the mortgage, utilities, etc. by herself? My emotions were everywhere like a broken faucet. I proceeded to call my best girlfriend because at this point, I knew I was losing my mind. I remember shouting out loud, "I" don't know if I can do this. "I" don't know where to start. Where will I move my family to live? THIS, THIS is too hard. Y'all don't understand. I have never been alone. "I" cannnn't, I cannnn't do this. At that moment, silence filled the air. I could hear a soft voice.…Angie, sis, YOU have to do this. This is your time to have freedom, freedom from a toxic marriage where L-O-V-E has failed you. Honee, I know this is painful, but YOU have to let go so you can *grow* through this pain! The other side I promise sis is going to bring you peace, joy and happiness beyond what you have right now. So, trust the process. It will not fail you. Just know your sistahs are here for YOU on whatever choice you make. In that moment my heart paused. "I" could only imagine how Lazarus felt. When it seems GOD is doing nothing, HE is doing more than you can ever imagine so HE can be glorified in the end!

I continued my normal routine. Go to work, come home and back to work again, stop by the grocery store than back home trying to keep it all together. I found solace in being with my patients daily, mentally escaping to another world away from what had been familiar to me...my marital home. I started finding peace in appreciating the season "I" was in. It was there "I" began discovering the most about who "I" was and comfortable in letting the journey unfold. Journaling would be my new outlet and my voice of reason. See I never used my voice. Growing up in my parent's home my voice did not exist, and my feelings were not validated. Same in my marriage. I never exercised my voice in my marriage. I was a wife, mother, friend and an employee. So here I am at 43 years of age trying to figure this sh?t out. The first thing I wrote in my new journal at the top of the page was my grandmother's favorite word.... Obedience! I would know later in life why this word was so significant. I finally surrendered to my new journey. It is now February 2007 and GOD's plan is in motion. Empowerment can come from any source. My source at this time would be the song by Mary J. Blige, (*not gon' cry*) my personal anthem. I kept it on replay in my car. It gave me life!

I called an Attorney and scheduled an appointment to file chapter 7 bankruptcy to stall the process of foreclosure until I was able to sell the house. The process was dehumanizing on every level. I felt violated by falsehood as if someone promised me something but never delivered on the goods. No this wasn't a dream I was having, but rather a freaking nightmare of reality. GOD was showing me what I needed to see so I could hear his voice and gain my POWER! It takes a lot of strength to walk away and let go! I left the attorney's office and mustered up enough nerve to secure a 3BR- 2 BA rental townhouse in a decent neighborhood. It would be closer to work for me. The children had their own cars and jobs which took a load off of me and my pocketbook. Spring is the perfect time for new beginnings. I started breaking down "the" house packing my life away. On this particular day at work my unit manager handed me a letter. I open it and it states the hospital has received a grant for all LPN's to return to school to obtain their RN degree. As I am reading the letter, I am distracted by one of my coworkers who ask me are you and your husband moving into a new house? I respond to my coworker with a fake smile and a big yes, we are! If only she knew the real story, she would be shocked. I finish reading the letter. I hear you GOD! Enrolling! My divorce attorney called me with details and my court date. I put the house up for a short sale and it sold without incident. I place an order for a moving truck and movers to transport my delicate life to my new place. Dismantling something in my home every day was like ripping off a band-aid. Everything that was once intact was now undone. Photo albums with thousands of pictures falling out of closets ranging from pregnancy, birth, birthday parties, field trips, music recitals, slumber parties, basketball games, family trips and the kids high school graduation were now more precious to me than they had ever been. They were sacred! I found myself with a glass of wine sitting for hours flipping through pages after pages of photos, laughing and at times crying hysterically recapturing memories of what use to be will never be again. I am awakened by the sunshine coming through my window. I had fallen asleep on my floor like a newborn baby, my glass empty surrounded by my family pictures. It was the best rest I had thus far. I have to get up, get showered and get dressed to see my doctor. This was the longest drive I ever had to endure. The unknown leaves so many doubts in your mind. I started to question if "I" had done something wrong? Why was I not enough? What did I miss? Was I not sexy enough?

## DIVINE INTERCEPTION

I explained to my doctor what I had been going through. She agreed with me to conduct a thorough exam and order all tests she think I may need. My doctor was so accommodating and reassuring. I returned home and my phone rings. My divorce attorney calls to tell me to come by the office and sign my papers. I felt numb and I couldn't move. I could only reply with the word, "ok." This is really happening. I am going to be a "single woman" after 26 years of marriage. I'm not ready!!!

The court date came and it was the feeling of doom. As we waited in the lobby, I studied for my biology exam that I would be taking the next day to keep me from having to look at "him and his attorney." The liquid sunshine was painting pictures against the courthouse windowpanes. I faded into a fixed stare imagining what my life will be like after today, D-day. My attorney calls my name, and we enter the court room. The court proceedings goes well. Papers signed and it is over in 10 minutes tops. That was quicker than when I said, "I do." As I exited the courtroom the ugly cry began and drenched my face. But this time as a warm cleansing. I sat in my car for what seem like hours and added to the liquid sunshine as if it didn't have enough on its own. My sistah called me to see how I was doing? I said I think I'm ok? She stayed on the phone with me as my ugly cry continued. She stated you have my permission to cry honey. Finally, what seems like forever to her, she says it's been twenty minutes and we letting this sh?t go now. I let out a gut-wrenching laugh which I'm quite sure could be heard miles away. In that moment I recognize how valuable it is to have my sistahs in my life. The power of sistahs supporting each other is immeasurable. I had leaned on each of their shoulders over the years. But this moment was far too much for me to bear alone.

Driving home I stopped and grabbed a bottle of wine and proceeded to my new home. My very own place. I celebrated my D-Day by myself eating leftover cheesecake and listening to Gloria Gaynor's song (*I Will Survive*) playing in the background. I danced until I became exhausted. In that moment Angela had truly emerged. I had never in my 43 years stepped into this most valued position. On this day I took ownership and vowed that Angela would have a voice today and always. During this transition GOD saved me from what was meant to take me out. I continue to journal for it relaxed my mind and kept me sane. Through this event I finally figured out the meaning of my grandmother's favorite word **OBEDIENCE,** which means to hearken to a higher authority so miracles can manifest. I became financially independent. Making my own decisions was so rewarding, a feeling of self-preservation. All of my doctor's visits were in good standing. I finished college at the age of 48 with my RN degree and as Vice President of my graduating class! One year later I entered the world of travel nursing and I haven't looked back. The "nightmare" was to wake me up so I could hear GOD speak to me. My Divine Interception was already in GOD's plan. GOD gets all the glory!!

Nicole S. Mason is an attorney, mentor, international best-selling author, powerful speaker and executive leadership coach. She is the recipient of the 2018 50 Great Writers You Should Be Reading award. Nicole was recently published in the Chicken Soup for the Soul ® Book Series.

Needless to say, Nicole brings a great deal of education, experience and expertise to any project or partnership. Moreover, in addition to her business acumen, she is a dynamic speaker. She has the uncanny ability to connect with an audience, motivate the listener and push the audience to action. Nicole S. Mason is the businesswoman and the effective communicator you want on your project. She is an example to women that you can do whatever you set your mind to do...

Nicole is married to her college sweetheart, and they have 3 sons and at the time of this publication, Nicole is greatly anticipating the arrival of her first SugarBaby (the nickname for her grandson).

# Make A Decision to Be Well: Healed to Heal Others

**Isaiah 58:8 – New King James Version**
*Then your light shall break forth like the morning, Your healing shall spring forth speedily, And your righteousness shall go before you; The glory of the Lord shall be your rear guard.*

"Nicky, Ms. Georgia is gone." These are words that sank deep down in my heart of the morning November 2, 2005. My prayer partner was at my door to tell me that my mother had passed away. I could hear myself screaming to the top of my lungs somewhere inside of me but there wasn't any sound coming out of my mouth. My legs went weak, and I hit the floor. As I lay motionless on the floor, I could hear what was going on around me, but I couldn't speak. My prayer partner was fearful for me, because I was 8 months pregnant at the time. She wanted to make sure that I and the baby were fine, so she called the paramedics. Miraculously, my blood pressure was fine, and the baby was fine. I couldn't speak to the paramedics. The only thing I could do was shake my head. It felt like my spirit separated from my body. I have come to know that I was in shock at the news of my mother suddenly passing away. Shock is good, because it gives the mind time to accept and embrace a new reality.

As we start our journey together, it is important for me to start with the sudden passing of my beloved mother, so that you can understand the frame of mind and the heart space I found myself in. My mother passed away from congestive heart failure. My entire life was built around my mother and grandmother. I was an only child and an only grandchild. Seventeen days after my mother passed away, my grandmother passed away. It was a very devastating time in my life. I am a woman of faith and had been preaching for many years prior to losing my mother and grandmother. My faith was tested in a way that it had not been tested before ever in my life. The next several years would be filled with ups, downs, twists and turns that would cause me to dig deep within to find a new normal and a new level of faith.

About three years after losing my mother and grandmother, I went to the doctor for a routine visit. Up to that point in my life, I didn't have any health issues. All of that was soon to change. My bloodwork was showing a very high increase in my cholesterol, and my blood pressure was extremely high. The doctor immediately sent me to a cardiologist. Ironically, I ended up at the same doctor that treated my mother. Now, I thought I was strong enough to work with him, but that would not be so. Instead of me finding another doctor immediately, I made the wrong decision to just let it go. This would lead to more devastating news for me in the years to come.

As I tried to put the pieces of my life back together, my health did not get any better. At the time I could not focus on my health. I just did not have the emotional bandwidth or capacity to focus on my health and navigate the grieving process at the same time. It would take a few more years before I could work diligently on my health and to make any significant progress towards my healing.

In 2015, I felt strong enough to take a deep dive into what I would need to do to focus on taking my diagnosis of heart disease and doing something about it. I scheduled an appointment

with a new doctor. He provided a regiment of medication and a low-fat diet plan. In the beginning, I wasn't consistent with my medication. I would forget to take the medicine. The reality was I rejected the fact that I was under 40 years old and needed to take medication. It just didn't seem right, and I certainly didn't feel it was fair. But there wasn't anyone for me to argue my case to. The only person that I could turn to was God to make my case. I finally decided to be consistent with my medication, eat better and exercise. My thought was to do it for six months to see what would happen.

In the interim of me making an intentional decision to take control of my health, I had two encounters that encouraged my heart tremendously. The first one was an appointment to see an acupuncturist. My time with her was cathartic to say the least. As she gave me my first treatment, I could literally feel the energy moving in my body. Grief, in my estimation, is a very powerful energy. And, what I have come to know is that so many people get stuck in the process. I didn't realize how deep I was grieving and holding that energy inside of my body. When she told me that my heart was sad, I cried uncontrollably, because I knew she was right. After several weeks, I could feel the difference in my heart and overall, in my body.

The second encounter happened during a Worship Service. A prophet that I had never met came to my church. At the end of the service, he asked for people to come forward that needed healing. I went up to the front of the church for prayer with so many others. By the time he got to me, he touched my hand. I opened my eyes briefly only to see him blowing on my heart! I literally lost it right there, because I knew that God had sent him to pray for me and to encourage me in my healing journey. I had the opportunity to speak with him after the service. He told me that he could sense that something was blocking my heart, so as he blew on my heart, he sensed it breaking in the spirit. It is important to note that healing is both physical and spiritual.

When I made the decision to take control of my health, opportunities presented themselves for me to share my story with others. The first such opportunity was an opportunity to be featured in a commercial about heart disease. I shared my story for the commercial at 2:00 pm one day and at 4:00 pm a representative was calling me to tell me that the company was interested in my story. After a vetting process, the company flew me to Boston first class, had a driver waiting for me at the airport, hosted me at a boutique hotel, had a stylist for me, a makeup artist and scheduled a professional photo shoot. The commercial took on a life force of its own. It has a few million views online and has been shown on more than 12 media outlets. The pictures from the professional photo shoot were displayed in numerous newspapers, magazines and on digital billboards located in national airports.

Of course, I didn't have any idea that the commercial would have such impact on the lives of so many. So many people were reaching out to me to tell me that they saw the commercial on TV. It was a way for me to begin the conversation about heart disease with others, especially women of color. Shortly thereafter, I decided to serve as an Ambassador for the American Heart Association to share my story and that of my mother's. Working with the American Heart Association has afforded me the opportunity to speak with the Executive Board of the Association and other top-level executives that support the American Heart Association. I was offered the opportunity to participate in a training program called, "Couch to 5K," that provided a running coach to properly prepare for the race. The training program was sponsored by one of local news stations, so people were able to watch and monitor my progress. It was a very rewarding journey. Others have been greatly impacted by my story. Women have started exercising and making better choices for their health. I have used social media to encourage and educate women about heart disease and steps they can take to make better heart health decisions.

In 2020, I made yet another decision regarding my health. I challenged myself to walk for 100 days straight. Not only did I meet my own challenge, but I exceeded it! I walked for 270 days, cut sugar out of my diet for more than 150 days, and I continue to make intentional decisions about my health.

I have had two powerful experiences on this journey that lets me know that God sees me, and He is on my side helping me along the way. My participation in the National Institutes of Health Study on African Americans and heart disease and one of my final appointments I had with my cardiologist. I wanted to participate in the Study for a variety of different reasons. Mainly, I wanted to gain access to the different tests on the heart that they offered, at no cost to me. In fact, I was paid to participate in the Study. When I finally received the results of all the tests, the result was the following words: "No signs of heart disease."

Then, I had a series of tests at my cardiologist's office, including a test with special dye to "open the heart" for x-ray like imaging. I had been in the doctor's office for approximately 4-5 hours. Needless to say, I was tired, irritated and ready to go home. Just when I thought I was nearing the end of my appointment, there was an announcement over the intercom within the office paging the Doctor to a room. Well, unbeknownst to me, they were paging him to MY EXAM ROOM! What!? I was in the midst of a stress test, and he walked in with a look of great concern on his face. He asked me a series of questions, and my answer to them all was no. Are you feeling winded? Are you out of breath? And, on and on it went.

I began to get worried based on how everybody was looking and responding to the situation. I did what I know how to do – PRAY! I started praying and crying and asking God to help me. It is at times like that when those negative voices try to rear their ugly heads. You know the voices I am speaking of. The ones straight from the pits of hell. I heard, "You're going to die just like your mother." "You are not going to make it." I continued to pray.

After the last of the tests were completed, I went out to the receptionist's desk to schedule my next appointment. I was feeling dejected and uncertain. Right at that moment, the young lady who had taken the last set of images of my heart came to the front of the office, and she looked like she had seen a ghost. The color was drained from her face, and she began touching my shirt, as she asked me if I was wearing a necklace. When I told her no, she proceeded to pull my shirt back from my neck to check for herself, as she asked me if I was sure I wasn't wearing a necklace. When I told her no, yet again, she told me that I had to come back to the room to see the last image she had taken of my heart.

Well, when I looked at the image, I understood why she looked the way she looked, when she came to the front of the office. She was using the same intercom that had been used previously to summons the Doctor to the office, because there was a problem, to now come to see the miracle. On the screen, there sat my heart with a huge cross prominently displayed on it!! Yep, you read that correctly. The first set of images, before the crisis in the office, did not have the cross. But after the crisis and my series of prayers, God responded. Matthew 9:20-22 says, "*Then a woman who had suffered from a hemorrhage for twelve years came up behind Him and touched the [tassel] fringe of His outer robe; for she had been saying to herself, 'If I only touch His outer robe, I will be healed.' But Jesus turning and seeing her said, 'Take courage, daughter' your [personal trust and confident] faith [in Me] has made you well.' And at once the woman was [completely] healed."* (The Amplified Bible)

I have come to know that everything that we go through is not just about us. It is about us using our lives to serve as an encouragement to others. God has strategically placed me in a leadership position to so many women. He has allowed me time to work on my own healing, so that my witness is authentic and impactful. I am grateful for His trust in me to do so and to serve others in such a way.

Valerie Lawrence is a dedicated proud mom, grandmother and veteran who loves to make others smile and feel loved. She is so excited about this opportunity to share the story about her beloved husband, Eric Lawrence who was the love of her life.

Valerie enjoys cooking and spending time with family and friends. She still watches her favorite movies in her spare time.

# The Ties That Bind Us
## Together in Sickness and Health

"**H**eeeyyy Rooyyccee" I cooed on the telephone to my grandson. I loved Friday nights like this, when my grandchildren each competed for their turn to talk to me on the telephone. I could hear my two granddaughters in the background screaming "Hi Ma-Ma" while my daughter, Erica, struggled to maintain order: "Wait, you'll get your turn to talk to Ma-Ma.." I leaned back in my chair and pictured Royce's smile while he anxiously told me all about his day at daycare. "Mama Ms. Shelly let me play with the puppy, etc...."

I decided to scrap my plans to go sit on the beach with a few of my girlfriends tonight. It was almost 10:00pm and I was winding down for the evening. And Lawrence, my husband, whose Friday evening activities were as predictable as night and day, was chilling in his mancave after coming in from the movies. He usually left work around 3:00pm and spent two or three hours at the movies so that he'd arrive at home right around the time that I would be coming in from work. We would catch each other up on our daily activities and then mill around for an hour or so before heading to bed. I figured I'd spend an hour or so with my grandbabies and then I'd motion for him to come on up to bed.

Royce was still telling me about his day. I could still hear the other two in the background: " I wanna talk to Ma-Ma!!" But I swear, Royce's cartoon-like voice always won me over. I could've talked to him for hours. Finally, Erica had reached her limit: "Mommy let's talk on Facetime so all of us can talk to you." Lately, Facetime had been a more convenient way for me to spend these nights with them, but my computer was down and I had issues getting good reception on my cellphone. I reminded her, "Erica you know I can't pull up Facetime right now." I never understood how my children were able to get so much better reception than I did in the remote area of Highland Beach. "Mommy just put the wi-fi code on your phone. If you look on the cable box in Daddy's mancave you can activate wi-fi and you'll get Facetime." Wow! Just like that, the mystery was revealed to me. Wi-fi huh? I laughed when I thought about how long it would take me to read those little, microscopic letters and numbers on the cable box, but I reached for my reading glasses and headed towards the mancave anyway.

I pushed the door open, explaining to my husband as I entered his cherished "Atlanta Falcons" room "I'm not going to disturb you, I just want to loo-------" My words hung in the air and I took in the scene before me. Lawrence was sprawled face-down on the floor, left leg trembling, clutching an extension cord.

"You can see him now." It didn't take long before the Doctor walked into the emergency room waiting area to escort me and my children to the room, they had assigned my husband. I thanked God that both of my sons were home at the time and called 911 as soon as they heard me scream. Erica heard the commotion over the phone and rushed to the hospital to meet us, where all of us tried desperately to be strong for each other. The curtain opened revealing a team of Doctors surrounding the hospital bed that Lawrence lay in. Immediately I saw the droop on the right side of his face. Stroke. The room starting closing in. Stroke. I wanted someone to get our children out of the room, but they were holding me up. Stroke. The team of medical staff hurried about making calls, reading data. Stroke. Someone was talking to me but I could only get bits and pieces of what they were saying…" Washington Hospital Center"…"Surgery"……"Medivac"……" Crucial"……"Massive"……. I could only make out one word:

## Stroke

It wasn't until one of the ICU nurses discreetly placed a tube of women's deodorant on the visitor's chair in my husband's hospital room that I figured I should probably go home and take a complete shower. Until then, I had relied on the birdbaths in the hospital's restroom and apparently that was no longer sufficient. It was then that I'd realized how quickly the past week had flown by. Yes, it had been one week, and the words were no less shocking than they were when we arrived.

*"Your husband had a massive stroke"*

Lawrence was still under heavy sedation. He had undergone a four-hour surgery upon arriving the week before, a thrombectomy, to remove the blood clot. His team of Neurologists warned me that the first week would be the most crucial as the brain swells, then returns to normal size. Since he had made it through this stage, his chance of survival looked better.

The drive to my house for that first shower was the most memorable one I've ever had. I have never tried so hard NOT to go crazy. I knew that if I had a nervous breakdown while driving, I would have an accident, so I promised myself a breakdown when I got home. Yes, that's it. I would give myself the honor of a breakdown. I would destroy something. I would smash the dining room table and then maybe take the sledgehammer to the grandfather clock in my living room. Actually, the more I planned the better I felt. This made sense. My 56-year-old husband having an Ischemic Stoke didn't make sense. It didn't seem logical to me that a good man like mine should be in a hospital bed, paralyzed on his right side, unable to speak, or recognize his family. But taking a hammer to all of the mirrors in my house was perfectly logical. Yes. I would do it. I needed somehow to shatter this illusion that life made sense. I had talked it and walked it for years. Lawrence and I were a loving couple of 32 years. We served honorably in the military together, grew up together, raised a family, attended church, traveled, taught, bought, sold, and more than anything, we had fun together. How was it that my husband had a stroke? It didn't make sense. I needed to express this. I needed to destroy something, something of value. I was mad at the trick life had just played on us and I needed to get this out.

I pulled into the driveway and quickly got out of the car, intent on having a nervous breakdown with a sledgehammer. I wanted to get in the house before any of my neighbors, many of whom had witnessed Lawrence being ambulanced away, saw me. I ran into the house and headed straight for the tool box in the man cave and…. "HEY VAL…. VAL IT'S ME, SHEILA!!!!" It was my friend from around the corner, Sheila Caldwell. I turned around and walked back towards my front door, trying to figure out why I didn't hear her car in the driveway. I fully intended to ask her to leave, but when I reached her, she hugged me. I collapsed in her arms, slid down the wall, and from somewhere deep in my diaphragm came a gut-wrenching loud moan: "HE'S PARALYZED!!!" Sheila knelt right on the floor with me and held me. I didn't recognize my voice but I kept moaning, yelling: "HE HAD A SSTTTRRROOOOKKKE!!" "WHERE THE HELL IS GOD??!!!" "WHERE THE HELL IS THIS GOD THAT I SERVE??!!!" Sheila rocked me in her arms right there on the floor for over an hour, soothing me through every outburst and supplying fresh tissue. It didn't even occur to me at the time that while I was mad at God for being silent, he had sent someone to usher me through a mental breakdown.

I took a shower and drove back to the hospital.

I drove back to the hospital reflecting on the past 32 years. I met Lawrence while we were both enlisted in the U.S. Army, stationed in Ft. Bragg, N.C., in 1985. His first name was actually "Eric" but we referred to each other by last names in the Army. I just never began referring to him by his first name.

Lawrence and I were one. Everything we learned, we learned together. It was only after the first four years of our marriage when we realized that, as common as marriage is, ours was rare. It was hard to explain. You had to be around us to understand it. Both of us were extensions of each other. Our greatest joy was being with each other, and after 32 years of marriage we didn't just love each other, we liked being together. It wasn't something that we flaunted or intentionally sought attention to, we just knew that we were blessed to have each other and we were grateful to God for it.

I tried to concentrate on the road while I replayed in my mind some of the challenges that we had endured though the years; the children, the deployments, both of our parents' deaths, relocations, new jobs…Wow.

I sat at a red light as I reflected on an incident that happened in 1989:

The Army had relocated us to Stuttgart Germany. We arrived at our new unit around 8:00pm on a Thursday night. Since there was no one at the reception center to process us in, the duty driver took us to a German Hotel downtown for the evening. After giving us the duty desk telephone number, he promised to meet us at 6:00 in the morning and drive us back to the base in time for the 7:00am formation. Of course, we overslept and didn't make it downstairs to the agreed meeting place until after 6:30am. We were sure we had missed him. I pulled out the number that he gave us and found a telephone booth a few steps away. Only to pick up the receiver and remember that I didn't have any German currency. I slammed the phone down and went into full panic mode "We don't know where we're at, and we've missed our ride!" Lawrence was still looking up the street for the duty driver. I got more agitated. "Why are you still looking for him? Can't you see that we've missed him? WE'RE GOING TO BE LATE FOR OUR FIRST FORMATION IN A NEW UNIT, LAWRENCE!!!" He stopped looking at the street and turned to face me. His voice was mellow and soothing, but stern: "Calm down baby, it's not that bad. We're just in a place we've never been before, but we'll learn what to do." I didn't realize it then, but those same simple words would anchor us through many of our years. "We're in a place we've never been before, but we'll learn what to do."

I focused my attention back on the road as I let the words from that memory comfort me: "We're in a place we've never been before, we'll learn what to do."

Two days later Lawrence's eyes opened for the first time since he had been in the ICU. He looked around as if he was taking in his surroundings. I signaled to the Doctor at the front desk to come in the room. I wanted him to confirm whether or not Lawrence recognized me, whether the part of his brain that controlled memory was affected. Before he even made it in, however, I had my answer. When Lawrence's eyes found me, standing right there on the left side of his bed, they started tearing up. I put my hand in his and he gripped it back. We stayed that way for a few minutes, crying and staring at each other. And then I spoke the words that have anchored us through so much: "We're in a place we've never been before, but we'll learn what to do."

If we thought the 32 years that we had already shared were precious, the months that followed were the most momentous of all. To say that our new lifestyle required some adjustments would be an understatement, but because we still had each other it was bearable. As painful as it was facing the reality that Lawrence could no longer speak fluently, it was as equally remarkable to know that we could communicate with each other without words. As many times as our new reality brought us to tears, we were nevertheless grateful that we could cry together. While traveling in a wheelchair had many challenges for us, we took advantage of the privilege of having assigned seats in the movie theater. We went every Friday night.

During some Winter evenings we sat in front of a blazing fire burning in the fireplace, while holding hands and grooving to one of our favorite jazz songs. During these moments we forgot about how our lives had changed and focused on what remained the same- each other.

I gained a new appreciation for God's word concerning marriage in this time. In Ecclesiastics 4:12 the bible says that "A threefold cord is not easily broken." With marriage consisting of a husband, a wife, and God, that cord is as durable as ever. Even when our human conditions -which are subject to imperfections- change, God does not. And he keeps fulfilling his part.

*"We're just in a place we've never been before" - Eric Lawrence Sr.*

*Lawrence passed away on May 2nd, 2018.*

Janet (Madam) Sackey is a teacher in Tema, Ghana who enjoys going around the town gathering information regarding AbaatanyE (Parenting) TV series. She is also a current student, seamstress, but being a mother is her most greatest job.

She is passionate about sharing her childhood experience and teaching women and young girls about the impact of parental negligence and importance of self-worth.

# The Generational Impact of Parental Negligence

**A** personal interview with Madam Janet Sackey residing in Tema, Ghana.

**Delayna**: Your personal story is powerful. Share some impactful moments and experiences of your childhood.

**Madam Sackey**: I am so glad for such a platform and of course this opportunity to have a meeting with prominent people like yourself. So, I thank you for that.

My childhood memories are impacted by several incidences. Let me take the positive and negative approach. With the positive I was the type that I like learning, I was academically good, so I always wanted to be ahead of time and I ahead of my friends. Since I've always enjoyed learning, I encouraged my classmates around me to also do the same. I like writing stories, acting, and drama. It was how I spent my time while I was learning. I knew that if I could do it, my friends can as well. And if I'm not mistaken, all my best friends (since we were five) are hard-working as well. They have a place of their own and they can now say they are real women!

The negative moments and memories of my childhood is that I suffered parental negligence. I never had the love of a mother nor the love of a father. Nor the love of my immediate family that was supposed to show me some sense of love so I was always like, even if I do something good there's nobody to go to and share the good news with. If there's something worrying me there was nobody to go to and explain my grievances or receive guidance. This was very hurtful and left me feeling sad and alone on most days. I should've been feeling happy that I was doing so well in my studies and schoolwork. Instead, I was often left feeling sad and alone because of this problem.

**Delayna:** You seem very passionate about embracing self-worth. Explain the importance of self-worth and achieving success.

**Madam Sackey:** Before I can talk about how self-worth has played a role in somebody's life or even my life, it is important that you have to know the meaning of self-worth. First, you've got to know that everyone has self-worth! I believe it is the opinion you have about yourself and the value you place on yourself! Despite feeling unloved as a child, I didn't allow that situation to impact my self-worth or self-esteem. Instead, I allowed myself to create a mental picture of what I wanted my life to be like and began working very hard to do everything I could to make it happen and achieve it.

**Delayna**: When did you decide to take back your personal power?

**Madam Sackey**: I decided to take back my power when I realized that because of my parent's neglect I was seeking love from outsiders. I was even seeking love from my friend's family and no one will show you love the way that a parent is supposed to. I decided to take back my power. So, I stopped seeking love and caring from such people. And then I said to myself, okay I've been to Sunday school I know Jesus Christ and the Bible tells me that even if my mother and my father forsake me the Lord will take me. So, I stood on that word and used this to take back my power! This made me realize that I am not alone because God is with me.

**Delayna**: Tell us about the legacy you are creating.

**Madam Sackey**: I have seen that I am not the only victim of parental negligence. I've noticed and learned that there are a lot. I have also even seen that my parents, especially my mother suffered the same negligence from her parents. That's why she also transferred the same to me, so I have seen that now. I thought it badly, so I wondered what to do because other children need not go through this. So, I talk to parents that come to me with a lot of complaints about their children.

Here in Africa, there is this what I call "parents are always right syndrome" parents don't respect the wishes of the children. They're always imposing things on them. It's as if they (children) don't have any say. The parents tell them it's what I say and that's it. I try to explain to them even in my teachings, especially the girls who suffers with this parental negligence. I make sure they understand not to seek love from other people especially boys who are only interested in sleeping with them. I stress to the girls that life is not all about seeking help or love from men. Because some girls think men are sources of freedom from the home situation. I encourage them to seek people who are available to sit down and listen, especially their teachers. The parents need to understand that children must also have a say in what happens in their life. Doing this will improve the way families get along and decrease childhood neglect.

**Delayna:** What are your goals for the women and girls in Tema, Ghana?

**Madam Sackey:** I thank God I am having this platform and opportunity! I wish I could have a microphone to be in the sky and scream so that every other woman can hear my voice. I want to tell the women in Ghana and the woman out there in the world that they can be independent!

They don't need to rely on men before they can become who they want to become.

They should take away the gender-based victimization and know that they can rise up and do anything they put their mind to. We are women. We are proud. We are precious. We must have confidence because we are capable of shaking up the world!

Stay tune for my upcoming TV series "AbaatanyE (Parenting)"

Sheila M. Anderson (SMA) is the CEO of Execute with SMA; through administrative assistance, operational excellence, and process development, she assists overwhelmed business owners to no longer be responsible for their everyday background activities so that they can scale their business, gain sales and visibility, and increase their profit.

Sheila is also the CEO of a non-profit organization called Eliminating Excuses®. Eliminating Excuses® is an organization focused on assisting individuals and couples to push past limits (self-imposed and other) and accomplish goals they never thought they could in the areas of Finance, Relationships, Business, Parenting, and oneself.

# Eliminating Excuses
## While Going Through the Process

Have you ever thought about a goal or life desire and made a conscience decision to pursue it at all costs? That is what I have done my entire life; I would see what I wanted and then I would do everything within my power to pursue it. I never desired to have children although being a mother of five daughters have been amazing! There were times in my younger years where I thought that it was my sole responsibility to please my man. I felt as if I had to sacrifice as much as needed to make sure that my spouse never lacked for anything. It was not that I believed he did not have to do anything. My focus just was not on it. This unbalanced way of thinking is what I believe attracted both my first and second husbands to me.

When someone is not balanced in their emotions and are unable to communicate what they need, it is breeding grounds for manipulation and being taken advantage of. There is balance that everyone should have in their relationships, but early on I lacked that. I became better the second time around but was not prepared for the same type of narcissistic and selfish behaviors that would repeat itself for a total of 17 years.

Let me step back to the beginning. I married the father of my first 4 daughters a year after the first daughter was born. We met via the youth ministry at the church we were attending at the time. Our first-time having sex I got pregnant with our oldest. I knew that I was pregnant in that moment and I was terrified. I did not know what to do but he was very attentive and patient while waiting to find out if what we knew to be true, really was true. We soon found out that I was pregnant but decided not to get married just because of this. So, what we decided to do was wait until we were both in agreement with the decision that would affect the rest of our lives.

Shortly after having the first baby girl, we decided that we were done "playing house" and decided to get married. A year after marriage, we had another daughter. Now, I never understood the importance of prayer until I was in my first marriage. You see, I remained married because it was the "thing to do". You know, when you are a Christian, it is engraved in you, that divorce is not good. You should stay married at all cost. Now, I still believe that divorce should never be taken lightly, and you should be equipped with the tools to know *how* to stand for restoration, not just being told to stand.

Now, one of the things that I learned in my first marriage was that I was the show piece. I looked the part; I was intelligent, and I was fertile. All characteristics and elements every man wanted in a marriage, right?? Soon after the second child, I found out that those things were not enough. Every time I gave birth to another child, another woman was revealed to had been satisfying my husband. He was extremely selfish and always made excuses for his actions. You know the excuses; you did not give it to me enough or it was an accident, or I was lost and trying to find myself. All of which did not make the indiscretions hurt any less.

Shortly after the last daughter was born, we decided to take a trip to Florida to see if we wanted to make this marriage work. Yep, I stuck around for six years of off and on cheating with promises of it never happening again. I chose to forgive every time and worked to forget the indiscretions so that we could prosper in the marriage. You see it was extremely important that we stayed married; for better or worse ~ 'til death do we part. However, we were 7 years in and constantly finding ourselves hurting each other. The vacation was horrible, and more indiscretions were revealed during our time there. Upon our arrival at the airport to return to Illinois, we received a call that his mom had a heart attack and was in a coma. You would think that was an opportunity for us to do better – nope. A year later, he filed for divorce.

I did not take the time to heal from the first marriage. I was so caught up in wanting to be wanted that I jumped into another relationship shortly after. We started as friends and because we soon after crossed the lines of friendship, we found ourselves in an emotional entanglement that led to many physical encounters. I was not emotionally stable, but I was clear of what I did not want again. This second man was five years younger than me. We started going to church together and within a year he was secretly meeting with the pastor to receive direction for proposing to me.

He met my children one year into our relationship. He was very attentive and did not run at the idea of being a stepdad. I did not understand his past or generational make up. He had things that he never dealt with nor spoke about until we were married and receiving counseling from the men's ministry. There were issues he dealt with surrounding the lack of self-control that were pawned off as typical "guy issues". Within the first year of marriage, he cheated. He gave his reasons and we sat before our pastor at the time. He told the pastor that he was uncertain as to if he wanted to continue in the marriage but soon after decided to stay. The cheating continued and so did the blame and reasons why he did not stop. He did not want to file for divorce but did not want to be married any longer. It was an extremely crazy ordeal.

Now I know you are probably wondering, "Why are THEY making the decision to stay or leave? If they are cheating, why didn't Sheila just make that decision?" I know! As I revisit all my life's choices, I am confident in admitting I did not think about anything but honoring my marriage vows. I made a choice to marry this man and if it was time for me to leave the marriage, it was going to be with my hands clean. I never wanted to have fault in the divorce. I know, more dysfunction that I cannot make excuses for. Owning my shortcomings and acknowledging the issues I placed myself in were my strong suits. My issue was making excuses for the men that I chose to procreate with and remain with at my expense.

After the second marriage started falling apart, I quickly learned the patterns of dealing with men like this and I was determined to not fall into the traps of before. Those traps including constantly talking to people about these issues, only praying and losing myself in my children and other people's problems to distract myself. The first thing that I did was searched within myself to figure out exactly who I was. What did I like to eat? Do I really want to pursue this major in school? Did I want to return to school? Where did I want to work? Can I be alone with myself if I never experienced what I thought to be love again? Can I be confident in the next decision I made for my daughters and myself without the "Amen" from those I loved? What do I like to do in my spare time? All of these questions were important to my future and the process that I was determined to go through. I also searched myself to determine what I wanted to do for personal development. It is great to make the declaration of being a better you, but the challenge comes with determining what methods to use during the process.

I decided to write out what a balanced and whole woman looked like. What did I want my now five daughters to learn from my process and what did I want to see them repeat or tweak to aid them in their development? It was extremely difficult. I was a single mother raising 5 daughters alone. I had to determine what I wanted to do with my life for Sheila. So, the first thing that I chose to do was finish my degree. When I made the decision to call the school, I had the credits with, they told me that it would only take me 1 year to complete my bachelor's degree! Only one year! I had been out of school for over 10 years and one decision motivated me to investigate and then complete what I had longed to complete.

I also decided to pursue being an entrepreneur. What was it that I absolutely loved to do and would continue to do even if I were not paid for it? In asking myself that question, I came to two conclusions; telling people what to do and assisting those same people in accomplishing the things they set out to do. You can search for how I continue to do this today. These are only two of the things that assisted me in my process.

I said that before, to bring light on one thing and one thing only; The process can only begin once you make the decision to move to a different place than where you are right now. My process was full of valid excuses. I could have used all the things that have happened to me and the things that I have done to myself and lost all ambition and hope. There is nothing worse than feeling like you are dying while having to live your life for your children because you know they would not understand if you gave up.

## My "Freedom"

I look back over every conscious decision that I made. I, like I believe so many of you have, cringed. The only way that I am and was able to make it through was through the support of my village and the grace of God. I gained my freedom when I made the decision to follow through with my process. When I made the decision to be a better communicator and trust that those who love me will understand the boundaries that I had to implement, freedom reigned.

A hindrance to progress is overthinking the next thing. I was guilty of delaying my success because I did not think that I had time to pursue my needs and assist my family. The problem that I found with the Excuse – filled mentality is that time always got away from me. The excuses that were used were valid! I had children to train, I had a nine to five that I wanted to ensure I kept for the time being. I had a husband that needed me to help him pursue his goals. I also didn't know what the process looked like, so I excused myself from it based on limited information.

In the famous words of Honorable Nike®, "Just Do It"! Do not plan another thing! Do not outline another book! Do not meet with another business guru. You have enough to get you started. It doesn't matter if you start small, the power and freedom will come with the first step. Understand, this chapter is for those who know they need to do something but have made every excuse they could think of as to why now is not the right time.

It will NEVER be the right time for the over-thinker. Seriously think about that. Pull out one of your journals of ideas. Open your Notes on your smartphone or tablet. Talk to that really good friend that you continuously shared your hopes and dreams with. Ask them how long you have been telling them what you were going to do and when. If we are honest about it, some of our friends and family are tired of hearing us speak about all these ideas and doing nothing with them.

There will always be a reason (excuse) as to why you cannot do what you have been wanting to do for days, months and or years. None of them matter in the greater picture. Be consistent and disciplined and work to be known for your pursuit of your purpose in excellence.

Trust your intuition and success will follow. Tracey ReNay is a wife, mother, sister, serial entrepreneur, inventor, product developer, manufacturer and talk show host.

You see, I had to go through that season in order to prepare for this very season, my Triumphant Trailblazing season. I kept hearing and seeing those two words first separately then together, I couldn't figure out what was going on, what God was trying to tell me. Then in a dream it came to me clear as day: Tracey is Triumphant, Tracey is a Trailblazer, Tracey wears a Crown of Jewels on her head. I woke up from that dream and began to speak that over myself until I began to believe it.

This is when my journey of restoring myself, reclaiming my true authentic self, renewing my mind and body, strengthening my positive attitude, and began to foster healthy, genuine, meaningful relationships with those who love me for me and not some watered-down version of me or the version "they" have of me.

# Thriving through "Matters of the Heart"

**W**hew Chile, where do I even begin? Why is it that women tend to take on the mantra of being a Superwoman and operating as Superwomen in every aspect of our lives at the SAME TIME? Or who said we need to walk around always being the Strong one? Baby let me tell you; that gets exhausting. What's even worst is that often times we don't even realize we are operation in such a manner. We tend to move on autopilot operating much like the energizer bunny going and going and going. It was Sunday morning and as usual we were in church services. As praise and worship was going forth, I was led to the alter. While kneeling I cried like I had never before. You know, one of those uncontrollable ugly cries, makeup running all down my face. Just awful. The following Sunday I had the same experience at the alter just crying my heart out wondering what in the world was going on?

I had this overwhelming sense that some sort of transition was about to take place in my life. I had no clue what that meant only that something was about to shift and in a major way. I kept trying to figure out what was to come. This feeling went on for several months and then it finally began to unravel. You see I had no clue my life was about to transition in such a major way and that each event would be a test of faith and what I now call matters of the heart "literally" for me to walk through.

The first matter of the heart occurred April 2015 with the loss of my last living grandparent: my maternal grandmother. My mother was the eldest of her siblings and as such she was tasked with ensuring everything was handled accordingly regarding the home going service, insurance, you know: the final arrangements when a loved one passes on. As I mentioned earlier, I'm the strong one of the bunch and you guessed it I was there for my mother and aunts to make sure they were ok. We were all at the services celebrating my grandmother as she would want us to with lots of laughter, loud music and simply enjoying family and friends. Although her home going and repass was beautiful, I couldn't help but to think of the relationship I have with my mother and how she now must be feeling at the loss of hers. Talk about a matter of the heart. I had to quickly change my thought process because the emotions began to take over and remember "I'm strong" and had to pull it together for my mother I couldn't let her see me mourn. There's that "Superwoman" thing again trying to be there for everyone except myself. I wish someone would tell me where that came from. Shortly after grandma's services we celebrated her heavenly birthday with a balloon release all across the country. It was beautiful to see the videos posted from all of us. To see my mother with a smile on her face while she and my sister released their balloons in Chicago while daddy filmed was beautiful. It let me know that my mother was indeed going to be okay and that my heart need not carry that burden of worry.

Continuing on my journey of Matters of the Heart it's now October 2015. One Friday afternoon while sitting in the car talking to my middle daughter who at the time was frustrated about the coaches comparing her basketball skill level to that of her older sister. I shared how my sister would sometimes get frustrated being compared to me as well. It was at this moment the phone rang. It was my mother. While I'm trying to say, "I'll call you back" she says, "No Tracey I have to talk to you now, it's your sister." I must have temporarily blacked out because I had to ask my mother to repeat herself. She said once again "Your sister is deceased and I'm here waiting on the coroner to arrive" I remember falling onto the ground in my garage crying uncontrollably trying to comprehend what my mother just said. My heart sank. Now mind you while I'm on the ground my dad calls being his usual jovial self. My middle baby answers the phone on speaker. All I can hear is "Hey baby it's Granddaddy what's going on? What are y'all up to?, I'm coming to see you all soon?' She asks him to hold on because momma (me) is crying. Of course, as a parent we all want to know what's going on with our children even when they are grown with children of their own as was the case with me. I pulled myself together only to realize momma hadn't told daddy yet. Now here I am faced with telling my daddy that my sister is deceased. I'll never forget the change in tone of his voice. This was indeed a matter of the heart that was indescribable.

My heart felt as if it had just broken. My only sibling, my little sister is no longer here. How am I supposed to deal with that? Never mind me! How in the world am I supposed to help momma and daddy deal with this devastating blow of losing a child? I remember a friend came to pick me up and I cried like a baby once I left the house. I couldn't let my parents see me hurt because I know my hurt was nothing compared to theirs. The next few days were pretty much a blur. We kept trying to make sense of what happened. The Autopsy report would later reveal cause of death: Hypertensive Cardiovascular Disease. In essence my sister had a heart attack in her sleep. I blamed myself. I'm the big sister. I should've saw signs of this. I should've picked up that something was wrong. I should've protected my sister and I couldn't.

As if things couldn't get any worse ANOTHER "matter of the heart" strikes. My dad was admitted to ICU less than a month after my sisters' services only for daddy to pass April 2017. Cause of death: Cardiomyopathy a disease of the heart muscle that makes it hard for the heart to function and can ultimately lead to heart failure as in the case of my daddy. How could this be happening to me, to momma? What did we do to have to endure so much tragedy in such a short span of time? Talk about heart broken. My sister and daddy: GONE. Momma was so out of it she couldn't even handle going to the funeral home much less preparing the obituary. I remember my best friend picking me up just to get me out of the house. We went to another friend's house to eat and finalize daddy's obituary. Needless to say, I crashed out while my friends finalized the program. Side note: There's nothing like genuine girlfriends who are there for you no matter what. That's a "matter of the heart" for another time. Now here I am; heartbroken, feeling helpless having to manage the strength to be there for my mother who in the span of a year and a half lost her mother, her youngest daughter and now her husband of almost 50 yrs. I tell you it was nothing but the Grace of God that kept me during that time. This superwoman began to lose her strength.

So much had taken place in my life in such a short time span I was reminded of kneeling at the altar. I had that sense of transition and boy was I in transition. I felt like a piece of glass that had cracked in many places but was still in one complete piece. It was if one more ding hit that it would shatter in a million pieces. That's exactly what happened in September 2017 just five months after my dad's passing. My marriage of nearly 24 years ended. Now if that's not a major heart issue there for you! You marry someone, have babies, experience life together only to have it end. Truth be told we were never supposed to marry in the first place. However, like many others who are pregnant before marriage you do what's expected. You follow society's standard and you marry and try to build a life together. Wrong move. That life ended and ended in such a manner that if I shared it here it would read much like a movie fit for TV.

I recall walking down the steps of the courthouse after being pronounced divorced. He walked behind me. He asked me what my plan was I told him my plan was to take time to heal myself in an effort to begin to live life once again. He then says he wanted to tell me something he had never shared with me during the entire 27 years we were together. At this moment I'm wondering what is he possibly about to say to me. He looked at me through those dark glasses and said "Tracey, I love you". At first thought

I wanted to respond with "you did just hear the judge say we are divorced right" instead I asked why did it take for us to be divorced before you could utter those words. The response was that I should've known that he loved me and that he didn't come from a home that expressed love let alone tell those they love that they actually love them. To me that was a cop out. He'd been around my family all those years and saw how we loved on each other not only in words but actions too. How could you be with someone so long and not tell them you love them? Even worse how could I have held on for so long? That goes back to trying to live up to what society says. What a load of mess! I kept quiet because I didn't want people to know I was miserable and simply going through the day-to-day motions like so many women do.

We finally parted ways and walked to our cars. It was that moment that the glass I mentioned earlier that had been cracked in many pieces but still in one piece had finally shattered into a million pieces. Sadly, I wasn't crying at the loss of him. I was crying because the institution of marriage had ended. I had just become a statistic. I didn't come from a family of divorce or having multiple children from various men or any of that. I, Superwoman had lost all of her power. The matters of my heart had become unbearable. Or so I thought!

While going through counseling I realized that I hadn't actually mourned any of what I had just experienced. I had been on autopilot for so long that it didn't hit me until I was in the stillness of the room in the house of one of my Sorority Sisters' who so graciously opened her open to me after the divorce. After a couple months had passed, I moved back into the home I had purchased for us as a family. A big ole 3300 sq ft home that was completely empty. It was here that the healing process had begun. I truly believe God orchestrated all of those matters of the heart to get me to where he needed me which was focused back on him with no distractions. There was no one for me to be superwoman for. I didn't have to wear a mask. I was literally on the floor of my house just me and God. He needed me to get to this point so that he could reveal to me that which he's been trying to get to me all along. That it's not me who has strength to do or be anything but rather HIM who GIVES me the strength to do His will on earth.

I often refer to this season of my life as my "Valley Season". During this time, I kept hearing scripture Psalms 23 verse 4 "Yea though I walk through the valley of the shadow of death I will fear no evil for thou are with me, thy rod and thy staff they comfort me". When I tell you that scripture spoke LIFE to me OMG. I found a new church home that poured into me spiritually. What looked dark and desolate had begun to turn around. While in church one Sunday the Lord spoke to me and said: "Tracey you will reclaim, restore and ignite a revival in women back to a state of rejuvenation and renewal." At first, I didn't realize what he meant but then it all became clear. I finally felt a release to share my journey through my valley season I noticed women kept saying you give me hope, I'm so encouraged by you, I know if you came through I will. Yes, beautiful you will come through and begin to thrive just as I am.

That same Sunday in church I heard the Lord call me Triumphant Trailblazing Tracey ReNay. I now know he gave me that name for me to share with woman around the world that they too can Thrive through Matters of the Heart.

In 2004, Rochelle McCallister's idyllic life came crashing down as she abruptly became a single parent to 4 children after her ex-husband of 10 years was sentenced to 20 years in prison. After the initial shock, Rochelle went into survival mode working two and three jobs, at times, to provide for her children. Rochelle faced some of the toughest times of her life on this overwhelming journey. She felt devastated, abandoned, and heartbroken. But determine and focus to press forward. There was no time to feel, complain or share her pain. Instead, she made a conscious decision to **IDENTIFY** the areas of her life that needed healing & transformation, she was determined to **CONFRONT** the difficulties, and **CONQUER** them one by one.

Rochelle had a deep desire to share how she overcame the challenges of single parenting and is committed to improving single parents' quality of life.

In 2015, Rochelle married her best friend and the love of her life, James McCallister, who has lived the life of a single father and shares in her passion to help single parents. Together, they have a blended family of 9 beautiful children. Although her life has evolved, James and Rochelle are committed to helping single parents thrive in life.

# Gracefully Broken

Sometimes life is not what it seems. The life that we hope for ourselves does not always play out the way we envision. We imagine life as a fairytale and sometimes that fairytale can seem like a nightmare. We desire a nice corporate job, a big glamorous wedding, the beautiful family, and the loving husband. That seems like a lot of women's definition of true happiness, right? While it was different for me, I mean don't get me wrong, I had what I considered a good life. But there were too many instances of infidelity, abuse, and a lack of protection for my family. What seemed to be a fairytale in other people's eyes, was really a manifestation of a skewed vision of a broken girl's heart seeking love in all the wrong places.

Never healing the broken little girl, the remnants of the pain will manifest and dictate the woman you become, and the choices you make. It wasn't until I was married and had children that I realized that the broken little girl within me was running the show. I didn't realize that my perception and approach to life was skewed from the lens of a broken little girl's heart seeking love, protection and validation. Because of my trauma and unhealed places, I learned how to polish the surfaces of my tragedies with coping mechanisms that caused my life to look like a fairytale. As I revealed the hidden truth from my place of brokenness, I was finally released. The hidden truths, like being violated at a young age, caused me to protect my abuser, bury and mask my pain. For so long, I was emotionally unavailable. I suppressed instead of processed, and that became a daily fight to survive in life until I made the decision to identify what was holding me in bondage. For years I felt like a soldier on the battlefield UNARMED.

It wasn't until I was divorced, became a single parent, and sought counseling that I learned I had not forgiven my abuser. I was numb, unattached from my emotions and had mastered the art of masking. I was tired of the repeatable patterns, inconsistency, and all my behaviors and decisions were proof that I had unresolved issues. My unresolved issue was a hurt little girl, who had not forgiven her abuser, or processed her pain. As a child all I wanted was to hide and make the ugly memories go away. Nobody told, nor showed me how to navigate the abuse. So, I didn't know that I was broken, and needed healing. My unhealthy behaviors, coping mechanisms and decisions had dictated every aspect of my life.

The trauma of my abuse left me on a quest to receive love, protection, and validation, when I met my first husband, I just knew he was the answer to my prayers. I thought he was my charming prince who had come to help me forget my ugliness. I remember the night we met; I was at the Classic's Nightclub discreetly checking for a famous actor who by the way was Eddie Murphy who was seated in the corner of the club. I looked up to find a man full of swag standing in front of me. He introduced himself. We sat in the club and talked all night long. The night came to an end, the chemistry was perfect, neither of us wanted to go. He walked me to the car, gave me his number and he insisted that I use it. Even though we had an amazing connection there was something about him that just did not seem right. I could not put my finger on it, but there was something there that made me think he wasn't my type and as a result, I never called him.

Two years later our paths crossed again, the chemistry was still there, but still nothing...After losing contact a second time, we saw each other again and reconnected when he began to manage some special talent within our family. Reuniting once again, we became good friends and began dating. As time went on, we grew closer and began to do much more together. We had a son, we married, life was good, and I was enjoying the love, attention, validation, and other levels of stability he provided. Everything was moving at a fast pace. Our family had expanded and business was soaring. The first couple years of our marriage was wonderful until hell started to reign on the inside. Then things began to surface, and the plots in the fairytale started to shift. The abuse had crept its way back into my life, but this time it didn't look the same. The love and protection that I thought I found was gone. My friend, lover, and protector had become my opponent.

Never in a million years would I have imagined he would hit me, but he did. It was the first, and only time he ever hit me. It was like a scene out of a movie. I remember coming downstairs to him speaking to someone on a phone call, once he told me who it was, I felt it was inappropriate and a total violation of my trust. I was pissed off and wanted to talk about it. I stood in his face and repeatedly said, "you will speak to me now"! He repeatedly responded, "Not right now." We went back and forth 5 - 10 times "me now...him not right now". Then I placed my house phone antennae on his nose, looked him straight in his eyes and sternly said, "Yes! Right now." Within seconds I felt a sudden blow to my left jaw, I remember crying and screaming in disbelief, I looked in the mirror, my jaw was hanging, I could not even see my teeth. I remember being in total shock. My thoughts were scattered. I could not process what just happened. I remember screaming loudly, wailing, and incoherently calling for help. I remember my eldest daughter running to my aid, with a look…I'll never forget. She was so angry and wanted to hurt him. I froze for a moment in time. I thought all my teeth were knocked out of my mouth. I screamed even more frantically, I cried and threw anything I could lift at him. I do not remember how I got to the hospital, but I woke up there. There was so much blood in my mouth that the emergency medical technician inserted a suction tube in my mouth so I would not choke off the blood. I do not remember how, but I was transported to yet another hospital facility for surgery. My jaw had been broken in two places. As a result of the surgery, my jaw was wired shut for months. I was on a liquid diet drinking only from a straw, I used my hands to express myself, clapped my hands to get people's attention, and wrote messages to communicate my needs and wants. During those months, it was so overwhelming. That experience reminded me of that little girl who could not protect herself from her abuser. Once again, I had been violated, and my power stripped away. It had evoked feelings and thoughts that I had not felt, nor thought about in a long time. I no longer felt like that vibrant woman with the fairytale life.

I remember the day the wires were removed from my mouth. I was happy to be free from the wires. I was able to eat, and talk, and yes, gain my weight back. I was appreciative of the great support I received from my mother, my father, my best friend, and confidant who's my best friend and husband today. They made my journey sweeter than it looked and felt. My only reminder of that day now is the metal plate on the left side of my jaw.

After leaving the marriage, he was very persistent in getting his family back. After much consideration, I went back. Determined not to leave a legacy of divorce behind for my children was my heart's desire. Once again, I had forgiven my abuser, masked the pain, and restarted the fairytale again. The plot begins to thicken again and you would not believe what happened next.

Due to poor financial decisions, we ended up homeless. Yes, I said "HOMELESS"! The day my family was evicted from our home was a devastating experience I will never forget. The kids and I were coming home, and when we drove into the driveway the sheriff was at the door. They were there to execute the eviction which left my family homeless. Standing in shock and disbelief, I watched our lawn be filled with everything we owned. My home, my comfort zone, my safe space was pulled right from under me. I was in a state of unbelief. Once again, I felt like that unprotected little girl humiliated and scared. Who was going to protect me and my children? My family was being evicted, and I had no control to stop it. My mind was racing. What do I do? How do I cancel the Positive Women Uniting empowerment meeting at my home in a couple of hours? A thousand questions with no answers. Again, we have no home. As we prepared to get a U-Haul truck and figure out what was the next destination. We had some friends offer us their basement and we stayed there until we found a new home. It was a struggle getting back on track, after everything happened. We went from a 4-bedroom house, to living with friends in their basement for months. He worked hard to change the trajectory of our lives.

The modern-day fairytale was truly starting to manifest itself. Our family was living a life we never dreamed of living in the mini mansion with a winding driveway, custom made designer clothes, designer handbags, extravagant jewelry that included a 30k anniversary ring, and a new level of financial stability. We did not want for anything. We bought my mother a house, trips to the islands; closing down portions of the beach, on-call limo service, 18-footer boat, multiple garages and the cars to fill them, Jaguars, Land Cruiser, BMW, a nanny and a maid. You name it, we had it. But what looks like gold doesn't always glitter. Within a blink of an eye, we went from having access to the desires of our heart to a visit from the FBI.

A visit from the FBI...yes, I said the Federal Bureau of Investigations. I am sure you just sat up in your seat and said, "WHAT???" Well, let me tell you what happened next. He fulfilled his dream of becoming a millionaire, but with that dream came devastation. I remember receiving a call that changed my life forever. The FBI just invaded his job. Our bank accounts were then emptied to pay the attorney's fees. Shortly after the FBI froze our bank accounts and assets, came to our home, and removed cars. I mean literally driving them out of the driveway while we watched. The FBI was determined to incriminate him. My family's life was once again turned upside down and lives changed forever. With the FBI freezing our bank accounts we were unable to take care of our essential needs as we once did. Our security and family stability was lost. He was a high-risk taker, and his fall would be even greater. And after 4 years of uncertain hell, he was sentenced to twenty years in prison.

Now I am a single mother and every single material thing of value that I owned, had to be pawned to keep a roof over our heads and clothes on my kids' back. There was so much pain in my life, and because I did not know how to process it, I mentally checked out. Working 3 to 4 jobs at a time to survive for me and my family. My work was a distraction to keep my thoughts off the pain that existed in my life and my children lives. Parenting was very overwhelming, raising my 4 children single handedly. They needed my love, advice, direction, laughter, and a good time. I was emotionally absent, even though I was physically present. Trying to assist with navigating through life with their school homework, extra-curricular activities, preparing meals, relational problems, and more. Children want to feel attended too and attached to their parents. My children experienced everything with me, they were the purest of love in my life. I am so grateful that we all pulled through that unimaginable time.

Remember, I always polished the surface of my tragedies so I would not have to live in the reality of what was happening in my life. I learned I could not escape the pain. I had to really learn to process my pain. I allowed myself to become vulnerable so that I could identify the areas of my life that needed healing and transformation, I confronted what tried to destroy me and conquered my fears one by one. Saying YES and surrendering to God has blessed my life and it was the only thing that could rescue me from my pain. If I would have known then the peace of mind that comes with surrendering, believe me, I would have surrendered a long time ago. I cherish the experiences in my life, God prepared me in the darkest time of my life by first bathing me in His glorious light. Stripping away the layer of my pain, came healing and it released the broken little girl. She evolved into a mature woman in Christ, no longer looking for validation and protection in the wrong places. Now pouring into other women and showing them how to prune away hurt, shame and regret, trying to hinder their path toward PEACE.

After all of the heartbreak, something amazing happened. I was reunited with my best friend. Our two hearts became one and we married after knowing each other for 20 years. His Godly love, protection and attentiveness, means the world to me. We have A Love Beyond US, where our purpose is clear. I am also thankful for the family God has given us. We are blessed with a blended family of nine children and three grandchildren. I pray that you will allow God to give you your happy ending. The bible says that you're Latter Shall Be Greater. James is God's promise to me, and it is greater. Healing, forgiveness and starting over can be hard, but it is necessary. We serve a God of new beginnings. I believe in KINGDOM marriage, I'm a firm believer that man matches attraction, but GOD matches anointing. It is time for you to release your past and past pain. God is love, surrender all to him and receive your victory. The first step is making a conscious decision to IDENTIFY the areas of your life that need transformation, CONFRONT the difficulties, and CONQUER them one by one.

Because I was able to IDENTIFY, CONFRONT and CONQUER the challenges in my life. My healing allowed the broken little girl to become whole. My past no longer has power over me. Now I am proud to be living a legacy **that demonstrates strength, perseverance, and most importantly faith. I am a Godly wife and parent passing the baton down to my next generation.** The greatest legacy I will leave to my family is being the founder of Single Parent Achievers an organization dedicated to improving single parent quality of life. "I am" a life coach, teacher and motivational speaker. She is well (the broken little girl). P.S. I am living a legacy to leave a legacy.